MY LIFE IN THE
PURPLE KINGDOM

MY LIFE IN THE PURPLE KINGDOM

BrownMark

WITH CYNTHIA M. UHRICH

FOREWORD BY QUESTLOVE

UNIVERSITY OF MINNESOTA PRESS

MINNEAPOLIS ✗ LONDON

The University of Minnesota Press and the author acknowledge
Cynthia M. Uhrich's contribution to this project.

All photographs appear courtesy of the author unless credited otherwise.

Published by the University of Minnesota Press
111 Third Avenue South, Suite 290
Minneapolis, MN 55401-2520
http://www.upress.umn.edu

Library of Congress Cataloging-in-Publication Data
Names: BrownMark (Musician) author. | Questlove, writer of foreword. |
    Uhrich, Cynthia M., author.
Title: My life in the purple kingdom / BrownMark with Cynthia M. Uhrich ;
    foreword by Questlove.
Description: Minneapolis : University of Minnesota Press, 2020.
Identifiers: LCCN 2020023706 (print) | ISBN 978-1-5179-0927-7 (hc)
Subjects: LCSH: BrownMark (Musician) | Bass guitarists—United States—
    Biography. | Rock musicians—United States—Biography. | Revolution
    (Musical group) | Prince.
Clasification: LCC ML419.B78 A3 2020 (print)| DDC 787.87/166092
    [B]—dc23
LC record available at https://lccn.loc.gov/2020023706

Printed in the United States of America on acid-free paper

The University of Minnesota is an equal-opportunity educator and employer.

25 24 23 22 21 20   10 9 8 7 6 5 4 3 2 1

FOR MY MOTHER—
MY SUPPORT AND MY POWER

CONTENTS

FOREWORD

QUESTLOVE

IF YOU FOLLOWED PRINCE'S CAREER long enough and closely enough—and I did—one of the things you learned was that he was obsessed with duality. Everything was defined by tension between related opposites: right and wrong, good and evil, the divine and the profane. Even his hometown was a Twin City. So it only makes sense that BrownMark, who anchored Prince's band during its most productive and profound years, would write a story that depends on a kind of duality, where every movement forward is also a movement backward, where every attempt to preserve order falls into disorder, where success and frustration are bound together. Chords and discords, verses and reverses.

BrownMark's identity starts with a reversal. He was born Mark Brown and cut his teeth in the Minneapolis music scene, but after he was hired, fresh from high school, as the bassist for Prince's touring band, his name was flipped to BrownMark. His book begins with a different kind of reversal—one of fortune, with Prince's band onstage in Los Angeles in October 1981, about to open for the Rolling Stones. It's a big break, a support slot for the World's Greatest Rock Band. To say that the gig didn't go well is an understatement: it's one of the most notorious mismatches between opening act and agitated crowd in the history of rock 'n' roll, complete with catcalls and bottles heaved at the stage.

Enough reversals, though, and you might find yourself moving forward. BrownMark certainly did. He was talented and ambitious, and he was following the lead of the most talented and ambitious musician of his generation. BrownMark moved forward with Prince through the early eighties, trying to find his place within the court of the Minneapolis Genius. Was he a member of the inner circle? Was he a temporary thing? He was subject to Prince's whims like everyone else, on call day and night to record or rehearse, and that gave him a front-row seat to one of the best circuses of eighties music: Prince as ringmaster, trying to both tame and inspire the bands around him, including The Time and Vanity 6.

And then came the rain—the Purple Rain. Prince's breakthrough album, the one that established him as a permanent superstar, was released in the summer of 1984, and those of us who were tracking his every move couldn't help but notice that it came complete with an official studio band, The Revolution. The name wasn't completely new. He had hidden it on the cover of his previous album, *1999*, in mirror writing, but this was official. And right there, on bass, was BrownMark. He occupied that position for most of the next three years, which happened to be the period when Prince and The Revolution released a series of amazing records: *Around the World in a Day*, *Parade*, and *Sign O' The Times*. It's a half-decade stretch that rivals that of any other music artist in history: @ me.

But BrownMark's time with Prince wasn't done reversing. While he was working his day job, he was also launching a side project, Mazarati, which he stocked with musicians he had played with back in Minneapolis. He wrote for the band, produced their songs, served as their art director, and even managed to bring them into the Prince camp, to get them signed to Prince's new label, Paisley Park, where they had a chance to record songs written by Prince himself. When the group's self-titled debut came out in March 1986, with a mysterious cover image that looked like a cross between Flashdance and Tron, Prince obsessives ran out and bought it. I was one of them, of course. I listened to "Players' Ball," the first track (written by BrownMark), and "100 MPH," the first single (written by Prince). But Mazarati is better known for the Prince songs that got away. They passed on a song called "Jerk Out" only to have it resurface as a huge hit for The Time a few years later. And they were given an acoustic demo called "Kiss" and worked it into something starker and stranger, only to have Prince snatch it back and record it as his own. Remember that one?

But having "Kiss" repossessed was only part of the problem. Prince, ever restless, proceeding at the speed of genius, fired his entire band as he worked on *Sign O' The Times*. Brown-Mark's time in the kingdom was over.

This isn't a long story, not in years. Much of it takes place between 1981 and 1986. But it's a deep story. It's a story of low notes and high stakes, of Revolution and of evolution, of bands and fans and best-laid plans, of pills and thrills and daffodils. Hang tough, children, and read it.

PROLOGUE

BREATHE, MAN, BREATHE, I'm saying to myself. It feels like I'm underwater. The Los Angeles Coliseum's at-capacity crowd is so huge that I can hear the roar of it from inside the limo with the windows closed. The driver slows the car, rolls up to the security gate. I inhale deeply, filling my lungs. We've arrived.

The band looks worried. "This is a rock 'n' roll crowd. I don't know, guys, this is crazy. They don't know our sound." I tip my head back and look up through the sunroof where all I see is dirty-blue Los Angeles air.

I am so far from home. I can tell the sun has started its descent toward the western horizon.

We're led to rows of white tents all set up for different purposes: hair and makeup, press, wardrobe. The time is passing quickly with all the anticipation for the performance. This is Hollywood in 1981—and the biggest show I have ever been involved in. A production assistant comes to our tent with an announcement: "You guys are up next."

We're opening for the Stones. *The Rolling Stones—am I imagining this?* Only a few weeks ago I'd been playing for a crowd of fifty in a small Minneapolis place like the Nacirema Club or the Elks Lodge or Sylvia's with my band Phantasy, and now I'm going to perform with Prince in front of ninety thousand people at the Los Angeles Coliseum. A shiver runs through me. It's a whisper on my spine, a hint of something happening that is far bigger than I am. I am somewhat afraid yet very excited. I close my eyes and am filled with the feeling that we are standing on the brink of something extraordinary, something life changing, and I want to absorb every bit of this moment. I hear the drummer Z saying something to me, but what? I can't tell. Everything sounds muffled and strange.

Then I feel him tap me on the shoulder. "Brown, you all right?" I open my eyes. Dez, Lisa, and Fink are all looking at me, too.

"Yeah, I'm all right," I say quietly, smiling a little to reassure them.

I glance up at the sky again. It is scorching hot. I'm lightheaded and floating in another dimension. It's all so surreal. I see the Coliseum bathed in red light, and the sun is starting to dip toward the horizon. I can feel the warmth radiating from those walls—so massive, majestic, and imposing, so much history here. And now the sky is deepening, changing from red to blue to deep lavender, and the people are shimmering in the heat. Then the fire hoses are turned on them—they twist and cry with bliss, feeling the cool water as the sky melts into wet droplets of purple rain. Picture this. We step out on the stage. We are all on the threshold of a dream.

WHEN I WAS A BOY

AS A BOY, I lived for those sunny days when my transistor radio would pick up KUXL, a solar-powered radio station in Minneapolis and the only station in the state that, in 1968, played R&B music. It powered off at sundown. All the other stations my little radio with the tin-foil-for-an-antenna picked up featured music by the Beatles, Led Zeppelin, and Peter Frampton. The downside of living in Minneapolis at that time was that African Americans made up *maybe* 2 percent of the population, and the opportunity to hear any music made by black artists was meager, too.

My mother and I had moved to Minnesota because it was considered a safe place for families to raise children. My parents had married in the Bronx, and I was born there. Dad was a Marine, and my mother didn't relish the idea of moving us from base to base, so we left New York City for the Midwest, settling in a low-income neighborhood where we could be near my father's family on the south side of Minneapolis.

There weren't too many kids like me around. Most of my friends were white. I didn't think much about our different skin colors, though. Peter was my closest buddy at the time. I was so excited one day when he said he'd like me to stay over at his house. I told him I'd have to ask my mom. When I asked

1

her, she said it would be okay. I was elated. It would be my first time away from home, and I felt like such a little man. My mom wanted to speak to Peter's mom to be sure it was okay, so I dialed his number and his mother picked up.

"Mrs. Avery," I said excitedly, "is Peter there?"

I heard her slam down the receiver and then she hollered, "It's that nigger friend of yours!" I was six years old.

Tears began to run down my face. My mother held me firmly. "Oh my boy . . . son, there are a lot of ignorant people in the world and they're not worth your tears. Feel sorry for them because they're narrow-minded, stupid, and full of anger."

"But why?" I begged her for an answer. I couldn't understand the awful way some people acted, but I did know it was a bad word to use. As I grew up, I heard it from people over and over, but I grew stronger as a person with every hurtful comment.

After a while, it just felt normal to be treated that way by hateful people.

I was able to make friends who liked me just as I was and who didn't say mean things. They were kool. My very best boyhood friend was Michael D. He was from a more middle-income family; his father was a plumber. I'd go to his house every morning during summer break and was always invited to stay for dinner. His parents made me feel like I was a member of their family, even inviting me to travel with them. We'd go camping and fishing, and I never experienced any racism with them. I felt accepted and cared for.

And when times were tough, I turned to music to make me feel better.

Every day I'd wait for the sun to come up so I could hear 1570 AM KUXL play artists like the Temptations, Michael Jackson, and James Brown. My older sister Yvette and I would listen to the music crackling out of the radio at top volume and do dances like the Funky Chicken or the Popcorn, mouthing the words of the Jackson 5: *Stop! The love you save may be your own!*

We couldn't afford a television, so I didn't have a sense of what people who looked like me were doing in the world, but I did know they were on the radio. Their music spoke to me and my sister and made us forget (for a little while) the negativity that was also surrounding us. And that year, there was a huge struggle taking place in our country.

Because I listened to the radio, I was aware of the Martin Luther King marches, especially the one in Birmingham, Alabama, and I experienced the tragedy of his assassination. There was a lot of rioting on the north side of Minneapolis. I learned a lot on the radio about the civil rights movement. It was both an exciting and tense time to be a young black kid living in America.

In my immediate world, a mutual love of good music seemed to bring black and white together. Artists like Janis Joplin, Jimi Hendrix, and Sly and the Family Stone were creating music that appealed to all races. I would go to my white friends' homes to listen to music, and together we'd groove on songs that to me *sounded* like black music, and my white friends were really digging it. Listening to it on their large console stereos with big round dials and giant speakers was such an uplifting experience. I didn't even mind listening to the mainstream stations playing rock, country, or folk music because listening to it on their stereos was awesome—so crystal clear. Spending time with my friends' families had such a positive impact on my early experiences with music.

I made my first connection between music and sex when I met a new friend named Pat. Pat's parents were hippies: free-lovin', weed-smokin', drug totin', music-happy people who held big parties at their home. I was a frequent visitor to Pat's house. I guess 'cause we were just little kids, the guests and

Pat's parents had no qualms about doing grown-up stuff in front of us. Pat hated that his parents behaved the way they did: it embarrassed him and he'd always hustle me quickly to his room, because he didn't want me to see anything. Boy, did I get an eyeful! Adults would often be scattered about on the couches, chairs, the floor, quite often naked, or semi-naked, in various states ranging from asleep to high to intoxicated, and sometimes they'd be doing the duty with each other. I wasn't entirely certain of what was going on, but you would always hear moaning and groaning. But the music they played was *jammin'*.

My mom was single-handedly raising us and had to make a living to support us. I didn't tell her about the sights and sounds at Pat's house, because she might not have let him be my friend anymore. My mother often worked late, so we didn't have much time with her. My sister and I looked after our little brother, Michael.

My mom was always in search of a better situation for us—a nicer place to live or a better job. She eventually landed a job with the federal government, and life got a little easier. But she still had to work all the time to take care of the three of us. We siblings got to be really close, because in some ways it felt like we were all we had. We'd make our own dinner at night; Swanson's frozen dinners were easy and we loved them. We'd make hot dogs or peanut-butter-and-jelly sandwiches or macaroni and cheese. We were alone a lot of nights, but back in those days the neighborhood folks all looked after each other, so we had lots of "parents" who kept an eye on us. For the most part, we didn't get in too much trouble, but if we did, we could expect a beatdown by any of them. When I was coming up, parents disciplined kids without giving it a thought, and our neighbors would smack the living daylights out of you if you were acting up.

Being alone in that house all the time without Mom around

created some mental and emotional challenges. Seems like I was always looking for something to get into, and one Fourth of July, along with Courtney, Raymond, and Tony—some new buddies—we found something, all right.

That holiday we somehow got ahold of some M-80 fireworks. For whatever reason, we thought it would be funny to tie them together and then tape them to a neighbor's garage. We just didn't know how dangerous those things really were. We lit the fuses, then ran. KABOOM! They blew a huge hole in the side of the garage. The garage caught fire and burned to the ground.

I couldn't believe this was happening. Fire trucks roared up, and all the neighbors stood around watching. We boys were all pretty scared. We thought of it as just a harmless prank, but it sure went wrong. We were never found out, but I had a lot of sleepless nights worrying about that. I mean, we burned down a garage, for crying out loud!

There were a lot of good times, too. My mom would always find ways to pull us together as a family, even though we rarely saw our father. Every summer we traveled on the train to Chicago to visit my Aunt Bertha and Frankie. We'd laugh and play with our cousins as if it were going to be our last days on Earth. We'd goof off in their yard and we loved playing in the dirt. We would get absolutely filthy. We'd take car trips to Buffalo, New York, so we could visit Aunt Edna and my older teenaged cousins. They would always take us to family dance parties, the roller rink, and my favorite, camping trips.

Back in Minneapolis, when our neighbor Joffrey would come visit his grandparents every summer from St. Louis, we'd play war games and have rock fights and cut up until we were tired out. Joffrey was such a fun summer friend. I don't know what it was about being a kid but we loved to play in the dirt. We would picnic outdoors and bring a blanket and candy to watch the fireworks at Powderhorn Park. We went to the drive-in theater and watched movies like *Chitty Chitty Bang Bang* and *Lady and the Tramp*. We'd go to the circus when it was in town. Such fun memories.

One summer, we finally got our first really nice television set.

It was a huge cabinet with a record player, radio, and television all in one just like those at my friends' houses. Though we were now on the cutting edge of entertainment technology, we were never allowed to touch it except on special occasions. We grew up in a household where even sitting in the living room was outlawed. There was plastic on everything—the chairs, the couch—and even the lime-green shag carpet had plastic on it. God forbid if it were a hot day, because we didn't have air conditioning and all of that plastic would stick to us like glue.

New Year's Eve, 1969: my mother was up late watching her new TV. As she rarely had the time to really enjoy her television, she would occasionally stay up late after we were all in bed. Yes, bedtime was eight o'clock sharp. This particular evening I saw something that gave me a new quest in life. I could hear the music from my bedroom as they sang, "Celebrate, celebrate, dance to the music!" The song pulled me up and out of my bed, and as I peeked into the living room, I was filled with excitement. I had never seen or heard a band playing live music before.

"Mom, can I stay up and watch this show with you?" I wandered into the living room rubbing my tired eyes.

She smiled and told me to sit down. I was so happy and absolutely blown away when I saw the drums, guitars, and glittering lights coming through the screen. I was fascinated by how all these people could get on a stage and create such a sound right there in front of me. It was as if I could feel every note being played. I saw myself there, right there onstage with them.

I didn't have a clue as to how these instruments made their sounds, but I could feel something drawing me in.

When the program was over, I went to sleep and dreamed all night about how I could do the same thing. The next morning, all I could do was talk about the band that I had seen on our new television set—Three Dog Night. From that moment on, I couldn't get enough of watching musicians. I saw the Jackson 5 on the *Jim Nabors Hour* and the *Flip Wilson Show,* and soon they were all over television. I was on a mission now. I wanted to be like Jermaine Jackson: he had that big afro and was just kool playing that bass and dancing, too. I didn't have money for a guitar so I made one out of a shoebox and rubber bands. I tore up my mother's garbage cans and put them together as a drum set, using the cardboard rolls on clothes hangers for drumsticks, and I made so much noise my mother threw me out. She sent me over to a local church community center on Lake Street where they had a drum set. There, I was able to take some drum lessons, but it was far away and I couldn't go all that often. I was frustrated—but I wasn't going to let that stop me.

That all changed, thanks to the Sears catalog.

Mom used to get the Sears catalog in the mail every year, and as a young boy with an inquisitive mind, my interest in the catalogs was the half-naked women in the lingerie section—an addictive behavior I may have picked up from looking at my friend's father's *Playboy* magazines. Being familiar with these catalogs, I remembered a section dedicated to musical instruments, and I dug the catalogs out of my mom's closet where she kept them. I waited until she went to work so I could snoop around for them. I looked at them over and over again, feeding my frenzy to get one of these instruments. I started to brainstorm about how I could actually purchase a particular beautiful cream-colored guitar—and I was willing to do anything for money. I kept imagining myself onstage playing with a band with this beauty on my hip (even though I didn't have a clue as to how to play guitar). All I knew was that this instrument was meant for me, and I was determined to get my hands on it.

I might be able to convince Mom to get it for me, I pondered. My plan was to clean our two-bedroom, one-bathroom house every day for a week. Knowing my mom came home exhausted from work every day, I thought maybe she would reason, "What a nice son! Let me get this guitar he wants," and this would launch me on my way as a musician. Boy, was I wrong. After doing all this work, I got screamed at for going into her bedroom! And to make matters worse, cleaning then became a daily routine not just for me, but for my brother and sister, too. Now we all had chores and lists. Everybody hated me. It was the Everybody Hates Marky era. My hopes began to stall. I decided I needed to change my tactic.

It was customary for all of us to sit at the dinner table and eat in the evenings. So one day I decided, *I'm just going to ask her to purchase this guitar for me . . . what's the worst that can happen?* Just as we were digging into our pork and beans with sliced hot dogs, I took a deep breath and said, "Mom, I want to start playing guitar." To my surprise, she was excited.

"That is a great idea, Mark. I think you should learn to play the guitar." She smiled at me—this was really working. I was so happy! She felt that music was good for the mind and that learning to play would broaden my thinking. With excitement, I continued, "I tore this page out of the Sears catalog. It's the guitar I want and it's only $237 with an amplifier."

When she answered, I felt my fortunes reversing. "That's great, Mark, now all you have to do is get a job." As she smiled and changed the subject, my grin turned to a frown. I was disappointed but started to think the next logical thoughts: *What am I going to do now? How am I going to get a job? I'm too young!* I decided to go to work, though I was only eight years old. I put on my thinking cap and suddenly had an excellent idea. When I was cleaning her room, I had seen all these stamps she collected. They were called Green Stamps, and you could save them up, lick them, stick them into Green Stamp booklets, and make purchases from the S&H Green Stamp catalog. My mom didn't use the stamps, but she also didn't have nearly enough for what I needed to do. I planned to collect enough and then sell them so I could finally buy my guitar.

The following weekend, I went to the Holiday grocery outlet in Bloomington with my mom and hung out in the parking lot, asking people for their Green Stamps. I just put on my puppy dog face and walked up to people like a poor soul and asked them to help me out. It was working, too—I was a little skinny kid with an enormous head. My head was so big it was hard to hold up. I had big eyes and I knew how to work them. But my excitement was short-lived. After what seemed like a year of my Green Stamp hustle, I did some careful math. I would be about twenty years old before I had enough to amount to anything. I needed a new plan. Something faster.

That's when I thought of Big Stan.

Stan was a giant man who would drive up and down the street every day delivering newspapers. I use the term *deliver* loosely. I saw that he always struggled getting in and out of the car to bring papers to the homes. Instead, he would just throw them and they would end up everywhere: on the lawn, in the bushes, even on the roof. This jumbo-sized man had a problem, and in me, I thought, he had a pint-sized solution. I made him an offer: "Stan, I'll run those papers right up to the door for a dollar a day." That was a lot of money to an eight-year-old in the early 1970s. Stan agreed to give it a try, but he gave me only twenty-five cents a day. I was fine with that. I figured I would work my way to a dollar once he got used to me delivering those papers really fast. I was so fast, he even picked up a larger route. I was up to a dollar in about a week because I refused to help him for less.

Stan would sit in his car and listen to the radio while I ran from Thirty-eighth Street heading north all the way up to Thirty-first Street. It was working out pretty well for him. Before long, he was paying me forty dollars a month. And once I had saved enough between Green Stamp sales and my paper route wages, my mother ordered the guitar for me. Now all I had to do was wait.

Every day the mailman would watch me follow him through almost his entire route. When he would get close to my house, I was waiting for him to go to his truck and pull out a long box. My box. After a week, he probably thought I wanted to rob him or something because of the way that I was stalking him. One day it finally arrived. I couldn't wait to get the package open, to get past the big industrial staples and packing tape. All I had access to was a kitchen knife, so I used that to start working the box open. I got impatient and chopped at it like a maniac—to the point of damaging the guitar inside. I pulled it out of the box and saw that I had cut through two of the strings. I felt sick and wanted to cry because I had waited for so long and now . . . but then it was all good, as I remembered how Jermaine Jackson played on just four strings. He was my hero, so I figured it was kool.

I plugged it in and started messing around but had no clue what I was doing. At that moment KUXL was playing "Let's Do It Again" by the Staple Singers. The first thing I heard was the *do do do do* bass line, and I loved it. I was so excited that I could actually play what I was hearing—even though I had no idea that it was the bass part, not the guitar part. At the time, I didn't know the difference between bass and guitar, but that's how I became a bass player.

Problem was I didn't have a clue how to play.

I needed to find a teacher.

In the summer of 1972, we started going over to my grand-mother's house every weekend for dinner. Around the corner was a small shop called Swanson's Music, across from the cemetery on Lake Street, and I made it a point to head over there the first chance I got. I loved seeing all the instruments, and I knew I was playing an instrument designed to have six strings. I really wanted to know how to play correctly. When I walked in for the first time, an old man by the counter was sweeping the floor. He looked at me and said, "How can I help you, boy?" I was afraid to tell him I wanted guitar lessons because I knew I couldn't pay for them, so I just ran out of the store without answering him.

The following week, I was right back there again, but this time I was going to see if I could spring up a deal with the shop owner. He was behind the counter smoking a cigar, watched me walk in, and said, "Why'd you run away last week, boy? I wasn't gonna hurt ya."

"I was nervous because I don't have any money, sir, but I want guitar lessons."

He just stared at me for a few seconds, then removed the cigar from his mouth and leaned over the counter. "You live around here boy?"

"No, sir, I come to visit my grandmother every weekend." I think he was taken aback because of my manners and demeanor. My mother raised me to be respectful of my elders, and this was a rare thing. He was impressed with me, I could tell.

"Lookie-here, boy," he said, "you come here every Saturday and sweep this here floor, and I'll give you lessons. Is it a deal?"

I jumped into the air a little. "Thank you, Mr. Wilkins, I won't let you down!" He smiled and I ran out the door to tell my mom what just happened. I was so excited.

As I started my lessons it wasn't what I thought playing guitar would be like.

My guitar lessons were great at first, but after a few months I started to get really bored. I mean, all Old Man Wilkins would teach me was "Old McDonald," "Mary Had a Little Lamb," and stuff like that. I thought I was going to be learning some serious tunes from the Ohio Players, Earth, Wind & Fire, or some Chuck Berry. *Something.* I was impatient and eager to move past the nursery rhymes. I wanted to feel the music, not read the music. I felt that reading music was hindering my creativity, as I found myself concentrating more on the sheet music than on what I was hearing and feeling. I eventually quit my lessons, and as time passed I eventually put the guitar in the closet.

DISCOVERY YEARS

BY 1978, WHEN I WAS SIXTEEN, we were living in an upper middle class neighborhood, still on the south side but farther south where the street numbers got bigger. Mom was making better money so things had changed drastically from just a few years before.

I had become streetwise in the years since I'd given up on playing guitar. My father had also given up—on us. He'd decided he didn't want the burden of a family any longer, and being without a strong male role model led me to forge some friendships that were somewhat questionable.

But one of the good guys in my life was Wally. He was one tough dude. Wally was my running buddy, and we hung out together all the time. He taught me about the streets and survival. Before I met him, I pretty much stayed within a small circumference of just a few blocks around my house. He got me out of my neighborhood and taught me I didn't have to be afraid of new places. We'd ride our bikes everywhere. We'd go to the Mississippi River and fish, bringing hot dogs we roasted with a propane flame. Sometimes we'd bring a radio and listen to music. We'd take the bus downtown together and explore the city. He was a senior, and as I would discover during my sophomore year at Central High, Wally had my back. He was like a brother to me.

When our friendship started, we were both interested in girls, playing music, and running the streets. Disco music was starting to emerge on the scene with its very distinctive sound that crossed over the borders between Black and White. For the first time, we could hear disco on mainstream radio as well as in the clubs. Black artists such as Isaac Hayes, Barry White, Donna Summers, and many others started to break down the barriers to places that were once only accessible to White artists. Before this, Black artists played R&B and White artists played rock. There were really no crossover artists with the exception of Jimi Hendrix and the Average White Band. Disco sparked my interest in music again and made me want to pick up my guitar and form a band. It was as if this new sound was a missing part of me and I could now see my future. I grew up liking rock and R&B, so this new movement to me had the potential for a mixture of both genres.

My sophomore year would be a turning point for me, a very turbulent period filled with much uncertainty, hormone changes, and pimples. But I now wanted to be a *Rock Star*. School was a challenge because I never felt like I fit in. Well, I really didn't fit in, judging from how I started to dress. It took a few years to figure out a style, but trying to find one was fun. I wanted to look the part of a guy in a band. I started with my hair.

I wanted to try this new procedure called Jheri curl. The Jheri curl is a type of no-lye perm. My sister's friend did mine. Basically, we permed our hair with rollers and—*voilà!*—Super Curls. The only drawback was that being African American we needed to apply a lot of Jheri curl juice—grease—to activate the curls. That activator juice got all over everything: clothes, my pillow, even the wall if I leaned my head against it. Can you imagine the combination of Jheri curl juice and the plastic on my mom's furniture? What a mess! I couldn't turn my head quickly one direction or the other because juice would start flying everywhere. While I was getting my musician look together, the only other thing I wanted to do was play the guitar.

On my first day as a sophomore at Central High, I was assigned a locker after first period. I was putting my books away and getting organized when a group of punks approached me and began bullying me. One individual pulled out his brass knuckles and started to punch my locker door in. Another put on lead-filled gloves and started to shadowbox near my face. I was sure I was about to get a beatdown. With a rush of adrenaline I was ready for whatever came next. I looked around and said, "Come on, you x#$!@%s, let's do it!" I took my foot and kicked the first punk so hard his teeth flew out. Then I did a roundhouse kick and knocked two others out while giving yet another punk the grip of death!

Well, it didn't exactly happen like that. I actually started crying to mommy in my mind, but I couldn't show weakness. Wally saw all the commotion from down the hall and raced toward us and broke through the gang of guys like a bowling ball. He told them all to back down or they would have to deal with him, even if they so much as sneezed on me. So these punks went their separate ways, and Wally looked at me and said, "I got your back, bro! They won't be messing with you anymore." I believed it, too. But I knew that would be short-lived. What was I going to do next year after he graduated? I knew I was going to have to find my own clique to hang with.

As I familiarized myself with the school, I stumbled across the music room. There was no one in there at the time because class hadn't started yet. I got a feel for the place. Wow, it was a big room. It had a stage and more instruments than I had ever seen in one place. Trombones, trumpets, pianos, and violins all around me as if a symphony orchestra had been rehearsing and the musicians had just stepped away. It even had glass sound-proof booths all along the back wall, each one with drums set up in them. It was a sight to see.

I looked down and noticed a Gibson G&L professional series bass lying on the floor and plugged into an amplifier. I had never played a real bass before. All I had was my cheap guitar from Sears, which was so out of date the neck looked like a bow. All I needed were arrows for target practice.

It was as if this bass guitar were a beautiful woman calling my name. I looked around and didn't see anybody, so I started to play. It was the most awesome feeling: the strings were really big and the sound was so clean and deep. I started to get slaphappy, thumping and pulling the strings as I had seen bass players do on TV. I felt as if I had been playing professionally for years. That's when I noticed at least fifteen people had surrounded me watching me play this bass. I could hear them saying things like, "This guy is good" and "He's bad," and I remember thinking, *How can they say that when I have never even played a real bass guitar before?* I didn't really get it at the time, but I had a natural gift for this instrument.

A guy named Eric owned the bass and came storming into the room, yelling, "Who's playing my bass? Get your hands off my bass guitar!" I put it down before he could see who was playing, stood up to blend in with the crowd, and walked out of the music room. The word spread quickly throughout the school about this bass player jamming in the music room. It wasn't long before people were asking me to come up to the music room during lunch and play. Eric turned out to be really kool, and he let me play that beautiful bass until I could buy my own.

I started going up there every day before school, during lunch, and after school just to jam with other musicians. Soon I was one of the most popular kids in the school. Even the punk bullies wanted me to roll with them. That bad crowd, however, brought me nothing but trouble. I started spending so much time hanging out that between them and my music I began skipping a lot of school.

Around this time I met a guy named Michael Magic. He was a saxophone player in a band called Cohesion, and he let me borrow his old Kingston bass, and we'd play at his house. Eventually we formed a band and called ourselves Private Stock. We practiced every night from ten at night to four in the morning—rehearsing in basements, garages, any place we could find. I felt happy. I was focused and on the road to making something special of my life.

CHAIN REACTIONS

IT GOT TO THE POINT where I wasn't showing up for school at all. Every time I missed, a note was sent to the house for my mother, but I knew she would never get it because she worked all the time to pay the bills. I was able to hide my report cards and lack of attendance throughout the entire year. It got even worse when I started needing money to support my passion—I needed better equipment, amps, road cases, stuff like that. I started working at the Town Crier Seafood Cake and Steak House, and from 3:30 in the afternoon until 9:30 at night I slaved in the kitchen, then I was off to rehearsal from 10:00 to 2:00 in the morning.

Around this time, some of my friends were trying to get me into the pimp game to make extra money. Their thoughts were that I could make easier money without having to work at the Town Crier. I was introduced to this girl named Candy and taught by my boys how to run game on her. Soon after, she wanted to take care of me, buying me stuff like gear, jewelry, and clothes, and looking out for me. She even told me she was willing to go to work for me and give me all her cash. I started to feel really guilty about that, though. What would Momma Vader think? Momma Vader is my mom. She was so mean that the boys and I gave her that nickname after Darth Vader from *Star Wars*.

I decided to walk away from Candy because I just wasn't raised that way. Candy, on the other hand, got so mad about my decision to leave her that she told me she was going to start a rumor around the school that I raped her and gave her an STD. Candy made good on her threat. She first started telling people that I gave her crabs. As I walked the hallways in school my friends would start scratching and laughing at me. She then went to the principal's office and told him this wild story about me raping her and giving her a disease. I was called out of class down to the office and confronted with these allegations. They had the rent-a-cop there, a social worker, and I don't even know all the other people that were there.

But no one was listening to me. I explained the entire situation to them. Besides, I was a virgin so how could I have done this? I think they were just using it as an excuse to get rid of me because I had such a horrible attendance record and stayed in trouble. I was expelled from school and told I would have to go to a school for troubled teens.

Candy felt I had abandoned her and wanted to make me pay for it. Some of the advice given to me on how I should have dealt with her just wasn't in me. I could never raise my hand to a woman. My mother and sister are women I cherish, and I couldn't imagine someone raising their hand to them, so how could I ever do such a thing to this girl? My mother went to the school board and fought with them about my situation and obtained a transfer. I ended up being bused to a school in a predominantly white neighborhood. It was a miserable, dark time for me. I was innocent. I hadn't done anything to Candy. I'd never imagined that a girl could retaliate that way just because a guy tells her he doesn't want to be with her. I was later exonerated when she confessed to making the whole thing up.

Ultimately, Washburn High was a good change for me. It

was a long way from home and my mother, and I felt I would do much better over there away from my current environment. It took me away from my homies, and I no longer had that negative influence to contend with. It wasn't long before I found the school's music room, and like a fly on stank nothing was going to keep me away. I started to hang out with a new set of friends but decided to concentrate more on my schoolwork and try to keep my obsession with playing my baby—my bass—under control. With some of my new friends—Hucky, Kenny, and Joe—we formed a little group so that we could audition for the Mil Wheels school talent show performing the song "Rapper's Delight," and it was a big success. My popularity grew quickly after that show, but it made me miss my old running buddies at Central High. I was determined, though, to stick with my plan to concentrate on my schoolwork. I knew that if music failed me I would need my education as a backup plan.

Meanwhile, I decided to work on my image a bit more. We didn't have much money—though I was still working as a dishwasher at Town Crier—but I had resources that enabled me to figure things out. I was so preoccupied with my musician image I even built a bass guitar in wood shop. Shortly after that I built an amplifier. I started going to school with my bass on my back to distinguish myself from everyone else. I would just walk around with it everywhere I went. It was amazing what I could do with my own two hands. People definitely started to identify me as "the school musician," and I think the attention I was getting for being a musician fueled my desire to become even more popular. I still had my dream, and I had the hustle to get seemingly impossible things done. Looking back, I'm grateful that we had arts programs in our schools.

I still had my band Private Stock, but when I moved to Washburn we started to fall apart because of my wanting to do better in school. However, the saxophone player, Michael Magic, and I decided to start a new group and call it Phantasy. We figured we would pick up some musicians from a different part of town, thinking maybe this would help us get more recognition around the city. There was a powerhouse of groups performing around the city, and we wanted our stake in that popularity: The Family, Cohesion, Westside Band, and Flyte Tyme, to name a few.

The new group we formed was very funky—and large, at a total of twelve members. We had a full horn section, two singers, a percussion player, guitar, bass, drums, and a keyboard player. We even incorporated a magic show into our set—whatever it would take to stand out. We rehearsed the same hours as before, and it was a bit of a challenge for me, because the new rehearsal space eventually moved to the north side. If this was going to work, I had to figure out how I was going to get there every night and be able to get home with time enough to sleep and make class in the mornings. I was the youngest member of the group, and I didn't have a car or a driver's license, so I reckoned if I could just figure out how to steal Momma Vader's car without her knowing, this would solve all my problems. Mind you, I was only sixteen at the time.

My mom used to keep the keys in her dresser drawer upstairs. She took the city bus to work every day to save money on parking, so this gave me a good ten-plus-hour window from the time she left till she arrived home in the evening. The plan was set. I'm not saying it was a good plan, but it worked. I would just tell her bye in the morning, shut the door, and sneak down the basement and hide behind the music equipment I had stockpiled down there. Then after she left for work I would go upstairs, get the keys, and drive to school. This way I had transportation to get to rehearsal too. I knew how to drive—I was a natural. Who needed a license? It felt bold and brilliant.

She never used the car except for the weekends, so I knew she would never even suspect it was missing out of the garage. It was a 1974 forest green Chevy Cutlass Supreme. I put my boom box in the trunk and rigged the speakers for sound. I was on fire! Sixteen years old, driving to school with sounds? Oh ya, the girls were gonna like this baby! Everything was working out so well until one day I slipped up. I had a car full of honeys and was cruising down 50th Street minding my own business when a red Camaro pulled right out in front of me.

All I could see before the collision was Momma Vader's big shiny belt whoopin' my behind. Bam, screech, boom! The car was toast. Thankfully, no one was hurt, but I knew I was going to be hurt as soon as Momma Vader found out. I was dreading the phone call I had to make—I had to leave the car at the scene because it was undrivable. I'm sure you can use your imagination as to what happened when I got home.

As the months passed I had figured out new ways to get to rehearsal. I had just turned seventeen and earned my mom's forgiveness and trust back. She saw I was working hard at my passion, music, and wanted to help me. She probably figured, *At least he's not running the streets getting into trouble anymore.* She told me she would co-sign for a car since I was working, as long as I paid the note and kept my grades up in school. I was getting my own set of wheels! I think she really just wanted me to get a car because she didn't plan on getting another one with the insurance money. Plus, I became the Vader taxi service. She had me running back and forth to the grocery store, the liquor store, the liquor store, the liquor store, and KFC, just to name a few regular stops. It was all right with me, though: I did wreck her car. My problems were over now. I could devote more time and energy to my group Phantasy now that I had Mom's support. The hustle was on. My car became the cash intake machine! I would charge people for everything.

I started hanging out with some of my old homies from Central again (not the bad ones), and I would charge them to just sit in my ride. It was a mustard yellow 1974 Malibu Classic, and I had it decked out with the latest stereo system, custom rims, whitewall tires, curb feelers, and tinted windows. I even had dice hanging in the window with green fur on the dash. You could hear me coming six blocks away. I figured, the more Negroes I could pile in my ride the more gas money I would make! I put a hitch on the back to tow stuff around for people—cash only. I even made a deal with the band. I told them I would rent a trailer and move all the equipment to and from the gigs for a fee. Then I worked an arrangement with the U-Haul guys to let me take the trailer for free and slip them some paper under the counter. I had it going on. I even built the band's light show in wood shop at school. Hey, the wood was free, and all I had to do was buy some electrical supplies and Cha-ching! I was rolling in the Franklins. (You know, the money.)

Momma Vader saw I was doing pretty good for myself and wanted a piece of the action. She became the band manager, along with Michael Magic's mother, Beatrice. We called her Bee. They formed the dynamic duo, and the band was soon taking over the Chitlin Circuit of the Twin Cities. We called it the Chitlin Circuit because black bands could only play black clubs, and they were usually little run-down juke joints that paid scrap wages. But they were getting us booked every weekend and even during the week. The money wasn't very good but the fan base was growing. We started playing proms, weddings, private parties, and we even played some outdoor concerts at Phyllis

Wheatley Park on the big stage. Every year a large concert was promoted by the black community, and people from all around the city would come watch the bands perform.

One day, we invited this bass player named Sonny to sit in on a few songs. Damn! This dude was the baddest bass player I had ever heard in my life. I didn't even want to pick the bass back up after this encounter, but I figured, *Hmmm, I could learn from this dude.* I became friends with Crazy Sonny. I called him Crazy because he was. Not only could he play bass, he could fight! I wasn't scared of anything when I was around this kat. He taught me a lot about bass playing and performing. I soon began to develop my own little style that people were starting to pick up on. I earned the name Thumper because I became well known for my slap technique on the bass. There were a few bad bass players around the city, and I was finally in the ranks.

THE SKIN I'M IN

MY STYLE, TECHNIQUE, AND LOOK were each becoming more defined. I still had a long way to go but didn't realize it then. I was only familiar with what I grew up around. Minneapolis was pretty much isolated from the rest of the world at that time. It was a Scandinavian Mecca. The black community was so small I thought I was a world-renowned rock star! I had high hopes and expectations and was determined to one day break out of the Chitlin Circuit and into the white club scene. I knew it would be a hard battle because the racism in the Midwest was very subtle back then. You didn't know who hated you because of the color of your skin. White people would smile in your face but call you a nigger behind your back. I learned in later years that it wasn't like that in the South. You knew right away who didn't like you. I prefer it that way because I like to know who my enemies are. The club scene in Minneapolis was no different; I couldn't even get into a white club, and if I did I was quickly thrown out for being falsely accused of doing whatever. This was a focused concern in white Minneapolis at the time— supposed black threats to white women. "Sir, we have to ask you to leave the club because it's been reported you are harassing some of the patrons." I didn't know standing up against the wall people-watching was considered harassment at Uncle Sam's.

White bands in town had the nice clubs to play in. But the beginning of the end of a white-only downtown Minneapolis had already begun, in the late 1960s, with the King Solomon's Mines club in the Foshay Tower, an iconic symbol of the city. When King Solomon's Mines integrated musicians and downtown nightlife crowds, it lasted less than two years and closed in 1968 under duress. Harassment by police, sanctioned by City Hall, forced its closure barely ten years before was I leaning against the wall at Sam's, minding my own business. Black musicians had been the driving force of this pushback against what was otherwise white-only, with police force actions continuing into the 1970s, and liquor board strong-arming well into the 1980s.

The nice clubs white bands had to play in had all the good equipment, the lights, the stage. All we had to look forward to was some homemade ghetto equipment and stuff we had on layaway at the music store for the past two years. Our stage was the floor with a carpet under the drummer so the drums didn't slide into the singer during a set. I can remember the only music store that sold live stage gear was over Northeast. Well, it was the only store I would dare go to. We used to have to sneak over there to purchase equipment, because if the neighborhood guys caught us on their side of town, in Polish territory, we would have to fight our way back across the bridge. Fortunately, I never encountered any trouble over there, but I had heard the horror stories. I don't know why the racial tension was so high, but I just learned to live with it.

We used to have problems with the neo-Nazis as well. They would get in their trucks and drive around South Minneapolis just looking for a couple of darkies so they could jump on them with their baseball bats.

When I didn't have the car, I would take the bus sometimes,

really late at night. One night Michael Magic and I were transferring buses on the corner of Chicago and Lake. We were sitting on the bench waiting for the bus, minding our own business, when five skinheads jumped out of a van with baseball bats and started coming after us. Michael ran off to find a stick or something to fight with. I have always been a man of faith, and that day made my faith in God even stronger. Alone in the moment, I started to pray in fear that I was going to be beaten to death by these skinheads. They had swastikas tattooed on their heads and wore black bomber-type jackets with military-style boots. They started to swing their bats and crowbars and shatter the fiberglass bus stand.

I put my head down and closed my eyes as if I were meditating. I didn't flinch a muscle, as I didn't want to show fear. As I was praying, they must have thought I was in some kind of deep kung fu meditation or something, because I didn't move when they hit the bench with their bats. I slowly opened my eyes and looked at the leader dead in his eyes and said with a slow but calm voice, "What have I to do with you? I'm sitting here minding my own business, and you want to fight me?" Straight out of the movie *Kung Fu!* Then I stood up and faced him as if I was going to do some Bruce Lee on his butt. Now I didn't know crap about kung fu, but I was sho-nuff bluffing.

The amazing thing was they all stopped, and the leader said to me, "We have no beef with you!" He looked at his boys and said, "Let's roll." When Michael came back, I know he thought I would be dead, laid out bleeding in the street. He saw me sitting there and said, "What the hell did you say to them?" I told him what happened, and we both began to laugh from the fear. That was my first real encounter with death, and I learned something from it. I learned that racism stemmed from ignorance. They didn't really know what they were mad at or why they hated me.

They were just some young racist skinheads looking for a reason to vent their own frustration. Why they didn't beat me to death I'll never know, but I do know someone was looking out for me. And it wouldn't be the last time.

NEW LOOK, NEW SOUND

ABOUT A YEAR LATER, while still working at the Town Crier, I was cooking in the kitchen and this kat came strolling in and sat down. He was really different looking, had a really weird hair style with this heavy punk rock look. I guess he was going out with one of the waitresses, Kim Upsher. I remember she gave me his order and said, "Make sure you do a good job on this one."

My left eyebrow lifted out of curiosity due to her assertive tone, so I said, "I do a good job on all the food I cook. What makes this one so special?"

She said, "You don't know who that is?"

"No, should I?"

"That's Prince."

I couldn't believe it! He was a kat that I had heard so much about among the local musicians, but I had never met him. He had just come out with an album, and I was amazed at the sound of it. I made sure his food was on point. I kept peeking around the corner and staring at him. I knew my image was going to have to change now. I wanted to look like *this* dude. The problem was where was I going to find clothes like that? He was wearing vintage-type clothing. Very feminine attire as if he went shopping at an old movie costume store.

I proceeded to make him pancakes with a special touch of vanilla extract added to the buttermilk recipe the restaurant used. I wanted to impress him for some reason, even though he wouldn't even know who was cooking for him. He just had an aura about him and I felt something in his presence. I remember him laughing at me because I was a bit obnoxious peeking in on him. I'm sure he could see my little uncombed afro jumping up and down so I could see him from behind the waitress station.

Immediately after my encounter with this kat called Prince, I started experimenting with different clothes, but nothing worked. Only women had clothes that fit the vibe I was looking for, but I didn't want to dress in drag. I started hitting up Mom's closet to see what I could find. It was a disaster. I found this plastic raincoat and a funky blouse, and I started wearing that onstage with some badly torn jeans and a bunch of cheesy jewelry. Soon it got even worse, when I started wearing fishnet stockings under the jeans. Talk about looking a bit on the crazy side. I didn't care—it was different, and that's all that mattered. I let my hair grow down to my shoulders even though the grease and the plastic . . . aw, man, it was bad, a true scary curl! Talk about Soul Glo! If I turned my head too fast, everybody was getting splashed. What was really bad was when it got cold outside. My hair would freeze and the grease would turn white! It felt like I was wearing a helmet made from KFC lard. The price you pay to try and look like a rock star.

The funny thing is, it was working. I started to stand out like a funky sore thumb in the band. People around town were even starting to dress like me. The problem was I looked like a rocker but we played R&B music. Oh well, I wasn't going to let that stop me. After checking out Rick James's new album, I was trying to find some platform high-heel red boots that would go up to my knees. Now that would shock the crowd really good.

Uncle Sam's (soon to be First Avenue) was the hot spot in Minneapolis at the time, the Midwest version of Studio 54. The punk rock scene was on the rise, and there was a little room called the 7th Street Entry where the punk bands would play. I would go in there every week to check out the groups that were performing. From what I was hearing, I knew if we changed up our format just a little, we could possibly get booked in this room. The problem was twofold: I first had to convince the band to reach where no other black band in town would venture musically, and, second, I had to figure out how to meet the club's music buyer, Steve, to convince him to give us a shot.

The very next rehearsal I came to the band with a game plan to make more money. My strategy was to convince them to play more crossover material, or Top 40, so we could move into a different marketplace. I didn't tell them about the club, because they would have immediately said no way. They felt as if we would never be accepted in this type of atmosphere. Music was changing, though, and with the new punk rock movement in Europe and disco at its peak, people were becoming more susceptible to change. There was a new music revolution on the rise. People were becoming more interracial, crossing over into a world once controlled by taboos. It was as if I could feel the change coming and I was determined to become a part of it.

But I still had to get through my last year of high school.

My first day as a senior was a day long awaited—I am shocked I even made it to twelfth grade. Even though I started to get my act together as a junior, I had done so much damage as a sophomore that I had to take extra classes during the year and go to summer school every summer to make up for it. I had received a total of fifteen Fs my sophomore year.

I was struggling particularly with one subject, history. I could not stand American history because to me it was very biased. I felt the school system never taught true American history; rather, it taught American selective history, if you know what I mean. I was tired of learning about Christopher Columbus's "discovery" of America when I knew he wasn't the first one here. Or how about Native Americans and how they were "savages"? The only savages were the ones who took their land and attempted genocide on an entire race. I also had problems with subjects such as war: where were the historical facts about the Buffalo Soldiers and the Tuskegee Airmen? And what about the War of 1812, when one quarter of the personnel in the American naval squadrons of the Battle of Lake Erie were black? I had learned a great deal about American history, but not from what the education system of the time taught me. So in my disappointment with the textbooks, I had a hard time passing American history. I knew my twelfth grade history teacher was going to fail me at the end of the year, and if he did, this would mean I would have to do summer school after graduation and settle for a GED. I was determined not to let that happen.

My schedule hadn't changed much from the year before. In fact it was worse than ever. I had to be in class from 7:40 in the morning until 4:00 in the afternoon. Then I would jump in my ride and head to Abbott Northwestern Hospital for work. (I had quit my job at the Town Crier due to financial issues. Can you believe after all my three years of dedicated service they only gave me a five-cent raise?) Anyway, I started working for the hospital as an assistant vegetable cook from 4:30 until 9:30 at night, and then I was off to rehearsal. Phantasy rehearsed from 10:00 until 1:00 in the morning. Then I would go home and sleep until 6:30

and start my day all over again. I think I averaged about four and a half hours of sleep per night. I drank a lot of coffee to stay awake. Most of the people I knew did speed, but I always stayed away from the drugs. Playing music was my high. I didn't need drugs.

Plus I had started crushing on this girl named Jayne. She was tall, dark, and she used to drive me so crazy. She was beautiful but possessive. Trying to juggle my time between her, school, work, and the band was insane! I had my fun fooling around with girls but never had a deep intimate relationship with one.

I was a virgin till I met Jayne. All my boys would have cracked on me if they knew I was still a virgin, so I had always hidden it from them. My first date with Jayne, she basically just took it. She jumped on me in the driver seat of my car, unzipped my pants, and was on me before I even realized what was happening. It felt like a violation. I've lived with that secret all my life. It's not the way I wanted it to happen. I was raised to wait till I met the right girl, until marriage. I started to develop a negative view of women, because all of my experiences with them had been negative.

It also didn't help that she was so jealous. One time she saw me with a girl who was only a friend of mine—I would always give her a ride home from school because she lived close to where I was going. Besides, she was a very big girl and had a hard time getting around. When Jayne saw her in my car she exploded. She tracked me down and made a complete scene in the middle of the street. Momma Vader used to always tell me, "There's only one way to deal with an aggressive woman, son: if she hits you, you hit her back!" She would never condone my raising my hand to a woman but in circumstances such as this she always told me that "if a woman is bold enough to raise her hand to you, knock her out!" Jayne started swinging on me like

Muhammad Ali on Joe Frazier! After a couple of hits to my jaw, I knew it was time to leave. We broke up soon after.

My weekends were totally congested. Momma Vader made me get up every Saturday morning at the crack of dawn to go out and cut the grass, pull the weeds, wash the windows, fix anything broken around the house, take her to the store, clean the bathrooms—and the dog! Mind you, I had other siblings! Why me? I don't know why she would make me do all this work. But I did wreck her car, right? I talk about Momma Vader as if she were mean, but she was a pillar in my life. She was tuff, but she only wanted the best for us kids.

By the time I was finished with my Saturday morning ritual I was off to work getting the band ready for that night's gig. We gigged every Friday, Saturday, and Sunday nights, so I had lots of work to do picking up the equipment and hauling it to the venue. I was the bass player, soundman, light man, and roadie! It was a tough gig, but it kept me busy. Being busy is always a good thing when you are a seventeen-year-old. Most of my friends by the time we hit sixteen were all into the ladies, but I was too busy for that. Having one girlfriend was too much for me already, and my agenda at the time was not girls. I think music served as somewhat of a shelter for me. I didn't have an interest in drugs, sex, and hanging out, which was really abnormal for a seventeen-year-old boy. I know that because of the way I dressed and by my attitude toward girls some of my peers wondered if I was gay. I think I was just so preoccupied with my music that between my goals and my time frame I just didn't have the desire to get involved. I didn't really care about what people thought about me anyway. I was in my own world, and I was on a mission.

There was this girl named Eve, though, who I took a liking to. I wasn't in any way going to let her know it. But one day I asked her if she was going to prom, just to see if anyone had asked her. She was a beautiful girl with caramel skin and big brown eyes. She went to Apple Valley High in the suburbs, and I knew my band was going to be performing at her prom dance, so I was just curious if she was going. Somehow she took that conversation as my asking her to the prom. I didn't have a clue this was what she was thinking. I would have loved to have taken her to her prom but didn't think I could pull that off, because I had to set up all the equipment and all that fun stuff.

The day of the prom I had called to see how she was doing and to see if she was going to prom. Like I said, I didn't have a clue she was thinking I had asked her to go. So she said to me, "Of course," and said she was going to be ready at 7 p.m. I was thinking to myself, *I wish I was the one taking her to the prom tonight.* All along she was thinking I was coming to pick her up at 7. As the night progressed the band was set up and ready to play the first of three sets. I was looking all over for her but didn't see her. We didn't have cell phones back then, so it wasn't like I could just call. We played our second set and by now it was closer to 10 p.m. I thought it was really strange she didn't show up. I found a pay phone and called during our second break to find out what had happened. That's when I found out she had been waiting for me to pick her up. Ahhh! I felt so badly after that. I was so stupid that I didn't even see the signs that she liked me and thought I was taking her to the prom. She was so devastated! I felt so badly I didn't know what to say.

There was no recovery from that one. She would never talk to me again. I wanted to explain to her that I didn't have a clue she was expecting me to pick her up for the prom, but she wasn't able to hear anything I had to say. I don't blame her for hating me after that. This was her senior prom and I had stood her up. Not on purpose, but still. She will remember this for the rest of her life. The sad part of it all was I really saw a future with her. I was just too blinded by my obsession with music to realize she was digging me. Music was my drug and I was addicted to it. After that I realized I had to find some kind of balance between music and relationships. I was too far removed from even knowing how to have a relationship with a girl, and I also think I was turned off by that disaster of a relationship with Jayne. However, when I met Eve it was a very different feeling, but I had unknowingly put a quick end to possibly a good thing.

In time, I was able to pick my face off the ground and get on with my life. It was close to graduation day and I was excited to get out of school. I didn't really know what I was going to do after school, but I knew that if music failed me I needed a backup. I was always interested in drawing and writing out schematics for my projects. I decided that maybe I should look into drafting school. If all failed I would still be connected to the arts through my drawings. I had to graduate first, and I was scared my history teacher was going to put an end to that. I wasn't going to sweat it, so I went down to the Minneapolis Drafting School and spoke with the counselors. They were pretty nice to me and basically told me I was in if I could pass the entrance exam. I didn't think that was going to be a problem because I was always good at math. On my way home I was feeling good about my future. I actually had a plan A and a plan B. What could go wrong?

As I was driving home I ran into some of the fellas at a stoplight. They wanted me to make a run with them over to St. Paul. They needed two cars because they said they needed me as a backup. I yelled out, "A backup to what?" They said, "We just have to pick up some supplies for this party and might need an extra ride. There's a 40-spot in it for you if you come along." I was always down for a hustle to make some extra loot. "I'm in, I'll follow you." We pulled up to this house and immediately I felt a bad vibe about the situation. I just sat in the car and waited for them to come out. There were four of them—Teddy, Corbin, Ben, and Tubbs. We called him Tubbs because every time you saw him he had a chicken bone in his mouth or something. He was always hungry.

They were always packing heat so that wasn't anything new to me, but they looked nervous for some reason. I was a bit on edge, so I started the car, put one foot on the brake, and the other over the gas pedal. I was prepared for a quick takeoff if necessary. They came out of the house carrying a really big case—a kind of trunk. I don't know what was in it, but I was hoping they weren't thinking that was going in my car. They popped the trunk to Teddy's car and stuffed it in there and went back in the house. Tubbs walked over to me and said we have one more trunk and there's not going to be enough room in Teddy's car, so we're going to have to use yours. He looked at me and said, "Relax, man, it's all good." *What did I get myself into?*

They brought the other trunk out and put it in my car, and Tubbs jumped in with me and said, "Let's roll." I didn't even want to ask what was in the trunks. I figured the less I knew the better. Tubbs started talking about getting out. "I gotta get out the game." I knew then I had something illegal in my trunk but didn't want him to see me sweat. I just turned up the music and followed Teddy to his place on the north side. After I dropped off the package, I was cursing at myself the whole way home. I realized right then how my association was going to drag me down into the gutter if I didn't break my ties. Here I just met with a counselor about my life and then I go make a run with these crazy fools. I had stopped hanging with them back at Central High, and I stayed out of trouble. I wasn't about to get sucked back in.

A week later Tubbs was shot to death during a pickup gone wrong. I had chills running up my spine. All I could remember was him telling me he has to get out.

I often think about how my life would have turned out had I not had my music to occupy my time. How many situations have I sheltered myself from because I stayed busy? I vowed to keep my nose clean from that point on and give up the hustling. Besides, I didn't need money that bad. Between my job at the hospital and the band, I was doing really well for a seventeen-year-old.

Graduation was finally here. I went to third period history class to see if I was going to be able to graduate. Mr. Butthead Snaggletooth, as I thought of him then, looked at me and said, "You can walk with the graduates but you will not get your diploma. I have to fail you because your makeup test was one question off a D."

"You're gonna fail me because of one question?" I yelled.

He said, "Personally, I just don't like you!"

I wanted to beat him down right there. It was just he and I in the class because everyone else didn't show up for the last day of school. He told me I could make it up in summer school and I would get my diploma at the end of the summer. I was furious! How was I going to keep this a secret? I would have to walk to the stage during the ceremony and pretend I got my diploma and secretly go to summer school so my family and friends wouldn't find out? I was crushed. I called him an asshole and walked out of the classroom. It worked out because I wouldn't start drafting school till the fall.

Then I lost my job at the hospital because someone was stealing from the kitchen. It wasn't me, but I was the token black, so I knew my days were numbered anyway. I started working at the 7–11 store on Chicago Avenue from 11 at night until 7:30 in the morning. This was really a tough shift because I had to change my rehearsal schedule with Phantasy (now Fantasy) to accommodate drafting school and working third shift. The band wasn't really happy with me. I was becoming more and more distant from them because I wanted to go a different direction from where they were going. I didn't know how much longer I was going to be playing music with Fantasy. There was a lot of tension within the group.

We finally got a call from Chrissy, Steve's assistant at Sam's nightclub. He wanted to set up a booking with the band. I had convinced the band to change up the set and learn some Top 40 music, and we set out for a new adventure with a brand-new audience in both the Entry and the Mainroom.

It seemed like in such a short period of time I had been through some very drastic changes in my life. I had graduated from high school, lost a friend and my job, started drafting school and a new job, and now had a new opportunity with my band. I was confused between drafting school and my job. I was worn out. I didn't know how much more I could take. I was hoping for the best with this club downtown, a club on the verge of becoming First Avenue and 7th Street Entry. If this was unsuccessful, I knew I would have to leave the band and pursue a career in drafting.

OFF TO SEE
THE WIZARD

HER NAME WAS TANJA, and I swear it was love at first sight. I was invited over to a friend's house one evening for a party. I wasn't there more than sixty seconds when I saw her. I had never felt that kind of power over me, but it hit hard. She could have told me to get on my hands and knees and bark like a dog, and I think I would have. She was up visiting from Overland Park, Kansas, and was in town for a week. I knew I had only a short amount of time to make an impression.

I started to develop a different appreciation for girls from what I had previously. She was different, and with someone like her I knew I could rule the world. She gave me power beyond what was normal for me, and I felt invincible. She was a freshman in college and we saw each other frequently. I would drive down to KC just to see her for a weekend. One Saturday I was driving around Minneapolis looking for a party. I didn't have a gig that weekend, so I was looking for something to get into. I was calling Tanja at her dorm but she never answered. I didn't think anything of it at the time but started to feel this really negative vibe as the night progressed.

Around 8 p.m., I drove home and went up to my room and just sat on my bed. Looking at this room I never frequented I felt for the first time that I was fragile. I started to tear up, and then the drops ran down my face. I couldn't understand what was going on. Momma Vader came into the room and sat next to me on my bed and said, "What's wrong, son? I'm not used to seeing you home at this hour." I told her I was really depressed for some reason. She says to me, "Have you spoken with Tanja today?" Then the tears poured down my face as I felt a darkness, a loss.

The next morning I called Tanja, and her roommate answered. I asked to speak with her and she put me on hold and went to get her. She sounded really different on the phone, and I knew right then something had happened. I asked her, "Where were you last night around seven? I tried to call you but you didn't answer." She didn't say anything back. I continued, "You were with a guy and you made out with him last night at seven, didn't you?" She was shocked and asked me how could I know this. I told her I felt it. I became depressed and went home and cried the exact time she met up with this guy. I don't know how I knew this but I did. She confessed to it. I was crushed because I had never been in love before. The pain was so great that I started to despise women and everything they represented. I felt they could never be trusted, and this had a serious effect on my future relationships. I became a serious playboy after that, because it was easier to deal with the pain, I think. Women became sexual objects to me, only useful for one thing.

Most of my relationship issues stemmed from growing up without a father. I never had a role model or an example of what real love and affection were really about. Everything I knew I had learned from the streets. Things were about to get much worse because playing music for a new audience opened the door to a whole new world I had never known. My world was no longer just Black—it was now becoming Black, White, and everything in between.

I was now nineteen years old and legal. The drinking age was nineteen back in the early '80s, and as a musician it came with certain perks. Just as I had predicted, playing in the white—and increasingly mixed—clubs brought us a whole new popularity. We were starting to develop a new following and new opportunities. The club manager was very pleased with the outcome of our presence because it was unheard of for a black band to be in these types of clubs. As long as he was selling liquor and bringing in people, he was happy. And Steve was happy to be going toe to toe with the liquor board over his belief that Sam's, and then First Avenue, should be a place where any person of any race should feel welcome and be shown a good time. Black artists and mixed bands continued to rise to the occasion and bring the magic into downtown clubs. Integration was happening, with or without official approval. That was the environment. The center of the pop culture universe was soon to be Minneapolis, First Avenue, and Prince—we just didn't know it yet.

One evening during rehearsal, Fantasy became embroiled in a huge dispute over the new sound and direction I was proposing. The screaming and shouting that ensued escalated to the point that one of the band members shoved my bass guitar to the ground and called me a pussy, daring me to do something about it. My immediate reaction was to stand upright, my lips pursed, my eyes intense, staring him straight in the eye to let him know that I was not intimidated. Despite my anger with what he had done to my guitar, I kept an appearance of cool composure, no fear. I did not want to fight, but I was fully prepared to defend myself if necessary. I could see the biting tension in his eyes as he looked around the room from person to person, trying to determine each one's intention, hoping perhaps that someone would come forward to aid his cause. But no one came forward.

His problem was that he had made the first move without carefully considering a countermove. If he backed down now, he would lose face before the group. And the worst thing ever is to lose face.

He pulled out a gun and threatened to pull the trigger. Life became a slow-motion movie in black and white. No colors. No sounds. No thoughts. No emotions. No past. No future. Just him and me.

I've read that war is the final stage of negotiation. When dialogue and reason break down, men are sent to the battlefield to fight and die in a bloody struggle to determine who wins and who loses. Differences are resolved with violence, the outcome determined not by who is right but by who is more powerful. Such was life in my world at the time.

But he did not pull the trigger. He laughed and slowly lowered the gun and said with a cool voice, "I didn't think you had anything to say."

His intent was not to kill me but to invoke fear in me. But I did not show fear. I think he felt that I was trying to divide the group and form a new one. Maybe he was just afraid of success. Like many of the older musicians around town back in the day, there was a reluctance to explore new beginnings and an impulse to retreat back to the old stuff. I guess when you are told enough times that you'll never excel beyond where you are, you soon believe the voices. They take a firm hold of how you think and feel. Slowly you begin to doubt your own abilities and accept your limitations. The future takes on the appearance of a forward motion where the hope and vigor of the young artist pass by the old has-been without him or her ever comprehending the transition. Life becomes a tragic reality moving swiftly to a place where talent and creativity sadly fade away into obscurity.

I was scared to death that the old man I would eventually become would regret the decisions of the young man I was that day. In life's journey we all have to face forks in the road as we travel. There is no way to avoid them. We have to choose to go to the right or the left. We must move forward. There is no turning back. Some of these forks have little effect on our lives, while others have profound, life-changing consequences. Our challenge is to comprehend the profound ones. This was a fork that was to have a life-altering effect. I understood it and was not about to let it pass me by. Even if I failed, I did not want to face my future old man with the regret that I didn't try. The irony was that this incident ended up dividing the group.

The members from the south side stood with me, but the members who lived on the north side were opposed to change. I can't believe it became territorial. It was very apparent where the allegiances were even though we all worked together as friends. I knew at that point that I was going to have to move on. I wasn't going to let anybody halter my progress. I was on a mission, determined to branch out to new horizons. But I didn't have to branch out too far.

# # #

A short time later, while practicing at The Way Community Center for an upcoming gig, someone knocked on the door of the rehearsal room and said, "Phone call for Brown!" We all looked at each other dumbfounded. Who could be calling the community center looking for me? The Way was a community center on the north side of Minneapolis where most of us black youths would hang out to stay off the streets. Our lead singer, Randy, was one of the community center directors, so we were able to use the back warehouse for rehearsals. We practiced in the evenings after the center closed at a time when no one was around. That's the reason why it was so unusual to hear a knock on the door and a phone call for me. I excused myself and took the call in the front office. I was a little apprehensive. Who could be calling me?

I answered the phone with a hard voice and said, "This is Brown, who dis?"

"This is Prince, and I want you to audition for my band."

I looked at the phone and thought, this isn't no G.D. Prince! "Now who is this? Quit playing games."

He began to chuckle and repeated himself.

Now I was completely silent, thinking maybe it really is the same kat I had cooked for a couple years back at the Town Crier. He repeated himself for a third time, "This is Prince, and I want you to audition for my band."

Everything around me became amplified. I could hear this high-pitched buzzing in my ear from the fluorescent lights above as the sound bounced around the room. *This can't be happening,* I thought to myself in disbelief. I couldn't believe what I had just heard.

Keeping my composure I cleared my throat, put on a deep voice, and replied, "That sounds cool. When do you want to do this?"

He said, "Tomorrow night. Does that work for you?"

Now I was about to piss in my pants! I pulled myself together and replied in an even deeper voice, "Sure thing. Where do we meet?" I had to force myself to speak with a deep voice to avoid sounding scared. Suddenly, it felt cold in that room and I was shaking from my nerves. He told me his drummer, Z, would pick me up at the 7–11 store where I worked and drive me to the spot. How in the hell did he know where to find me? And how did he know where I worked? This was all too surreal. He also told me to learn all the songs on his first three albums. Can you believe it? Three albums in twenty-four hours—how was I supposed to do that? I hung up and just sat there stunned for a few minutes. I didn't believe what had just happened. Had all my hard work paid off? Did I stand out so much as to have really been noticed by a celebrity? It felt wonderful that someone had noticed my talent.

I slowly made my way back to the warehouse with a blank look on my face as if I had just had an encounter with a ghost. The hallway back to the warehouse was different now. I was in a parallel universe, and the hallway had the appearance of a long tunnel that leads to a prison interrogation room. I was excited and scared at the same time. I knew I would have to explain to the band that I just got my break on the phone. *They will hold it against me, I know it.* I kept thinking the worst. I was reasoning to myself all the way down the hallway as if I were walking to my execution and needed to convince myself I wasn't doing anything wrong.

I opened the door and walked in as the band was arguing as usual among themselves while waiting for me to return so we could continue rehearsing. I walked over to my bass guitar and tried to pretend it was nothing. Everyone started asking me, "Who was that?" Randy said, "What happened? You look like you just saw a ghost." I didn't say anything because I knew it wasn't going to be good news to them. Just a few days earlier I had a gun in my face for taking a stand; imagine what was gonna happen when I told them this news. Without letting up they kept asking me, "What happened on that phone call, man? You're holding out on us."

Finally I broke down and told them, "It was Prince." There was a long pause. Crickets. You could hear a pin drop. "Prince?" "What the f— does he want with you?" I saw red eyes staring at me. It was silent again and I could hear my heart pounding. I replied, "He wants me to audition for his band tomorrow. He probably doesn't really want me, though. He just wants to check out my playing, that's all." It was so quiet you could hear the clock tick-ticking on the wall from across the room as all these red eyes stared intently at me.

You see, it's like this: I was the youngest but the most ambitious in the group. Most of the guys were much older than I was and pretty much satisfied with the way things were. At least that's what I felt at the time. I think this is why everyone was so shocked. Here was this young, skinny, freaky-dressed, long-haired teenager getting a shot at an audition with Prince when there were much older, more seasoned bass players available on the circuit. They were probably thinking, *Of all the bass players Prince could have chosen from around the globe, why did he pick him?*

Before I could do any more damage and tick someone off, I packed up my bass and left. It was already getting heated up as they were cursing and throwing things. I knew I wasn't coming back, but I left my amp and most of my equipment and I went home. Had I taken all my stuff with me I'm sure there would have been some backlash. I was a little sad because they were like my family. It felt like I was leaving a part of me behind. There was no turning back now—this was my shot and I had to make it count.

Michael Magic was trying to scare me by making comments about all the rumors going around about The Kid, as Prince was also known. "You had better watch out because I heard Prince is gay." He then told me that Prince was going to try to get in my booty as an initiation to join his band. I told him to chill with that. "You're just trying to make me scared so that I won't go to the audition," I replied. Out of all the band members, though, Michael and I were the closest. He was the one I would miss the most.

I knew I would be up all night learning three albums' worth of material to prepare for this audition. I put on a pot of coffee and dug in for a serious cram session. I had decided not to tell Momma Vader, because I didn't want to get her excited in the event that the audition should bomb and I would not be offered the job. In fact, I didn't tell anyone else. I just kept it to myself. No matter what happened, I knew I could never go back to the place in my life that I had just left. That one phone call let me know that I had what it took to rise above where I was musically and strive to reach the next level in my musical journey.

This whole ordeal was reminiscent of *The Wizard of Oz*, where Dorothy started off on a journey and was caught up in the twister that took her away from everything familiar. Following the yellow brick road, she set out to find the Wizard who would lead her to success. In her journey she would meet others who would travel with her. In my situation I found myself swept away from the only life I knew. Now I was about to take on a new adventure in which the destination was foreign and unknown to the only world I had ever known in South Minneapolis. Now I was about to embark on a journey to meet the Wizard of a Purple Kingdom and, perhaps, follow a path to a world I had only seen in the movies.

The sun was rising and I could tell it was going to be a hot and sunny day on the south side. I had been up all night working on Prince's music, "Bambi," "Head," "Soft and Wet," etc., until late in the afternoon the next day. It was time for me to go to work at the 7-11 store, so I got dressed in my punk rock attire (rather than my work clothes) and headed out. When I got there, my manager, Mr. Barns, looked at me and said, "You can't come to work looking like that!"

I replied in a matter-of-fact way, "You see, Mr. Barns, I can't work tonight because I have things to do."

"Well, then what the hell are you doing here if you can't work?" he yelled out. He told me that if I didn't stay and work he was going to fire me. I told him that what I was about to do I'd been waiting and working for all my life, and if he wanted to fire me, oh well, I'd take my chances. It was about 6:45 and my shift started at 7:00.

As instructed, I was waiting in the 7-11 parking lot for Z to come pick me up. He pulled up in an old Granada station wagon with wood side panels and told me to hop in. I wanted to drive my own car and follow him to the rehearsal spot, but he insisted. I was very nervous when I got in the car because he was a stranger to me. He had really long curly black hair and wore a thick mustache. He was much older than I was. The car didn't look like what I had expected. It was clean and well kept. No cigarette butts in the ashtray. No dice hanging from the rearview mirror. No torn seats. No roach clips. No dirty clothes. No smell of sex, drugs, and rock 'n' roll. The first thing he asked me was, "Are you sure you want to do this?" I was thinking to myself, *What the hell kind of question is that? Who doesn't want to hit the big time?*

Looking to the floor I began asking myself, *Why would he ask me that? I hope I'm not getting myself into something crazy.* I began to doubt the decision I made the night before. I was exhausted from being up all night and unable to think clearly, but

I pushed myself forward, thinking that an opportunity like this only comes once in a lifetime.

All sorts of rumors circulated through the Minneapolis music scene about Prince being crazy and kinky. Suddenly I began to wonder if they were true. I started thinking about some of the songs I had just learned, like "Sister," "Bambi," and "Head." The more I meditated on the lyrics of these songs, the more uneasy I felt. But this was the moment I had been striving toward for several years now, and I wasn't going to let it just pass me by because of rumors and questionable lyrics. Besides, I packed a pretty good punch and could defend myself if the situation got too extreme.

The drive seemed to last forever. Prince lived way out somewhere in a town called Chanhassen. I had never been to the suburbs before, and here I was out in the boonies with someone I had never met before on roads without a single streetlight. I could see the sun setting as we were heading westward into the darkness, which came upon us very quickly as Z kept asking me questions about my life and how I started playing music. I think he sensed that I was a bit uneasy.

I kept thinking about all the rumors I'd heard about Hollywood and rock stars behaving badly. It's funny how you can put yourself up on a pedestal and think you're a rock star until you actually meet one. Z was like this really cool hippie-type old-school rocker. You could hear the wisdom in his voice when he spoke. He knew more about the biz than I could ever have imagined. I felt like I was driving down the highway with Jim Morrison or Paul McCartney. He kept saying things to me like, "Get ready, man, because this is gonna be the ride of your life." I'm thinking, *The ride of my life?* I think all the rumors and stories put into my mind about Prince made me obsessed with the possibility he was going to try my manhood. This was all I could think about. Michael had told me it was going to be my initiation. I was sitting in that seat with my cheeks clutched tightly together the entire trip.

My heart was pounding as we pulled up to a massive black iron gate with armed guards and German shepherds on patrol.

Well, not really. It was a black chain-link fence with an electric driveway gate opener. But I had never seen a house with a ten-foot chain-link fence before. In the hood we had raggedy silver fences in the backyard, and the houses were so close together we could watch our neighbor's TV without using binoculars. We drove down what seemed to me a long, long driveway and pulled up to a purple house. It was dark outside, but I could see the property from the headlights. We hopped out of the Granada and Bobby shut the lights off. It was pitch-black out there! I was thinking to myself that if someone came running at me from around the side of the house, I would never see them in this darkness until he or she was on me. I could hear frogs, June bugs, cicadas, and other sounds I had never heard in my life. Nothing like the car motors racing up the streets with tires screeching as they turned the corner. There was no moon, but I could tell there was a lake behind the house because I could smell the lake water in the air.

We walked up to the front door and rang the bell. I don't know why but it seemed as if that door was about ten feet tall. The front door light popped on and the door began to shrink. This kat opened up the door and I stood face to face with Prince himself. At that moment I realized that I knew nothing (and I mean *nothing*) about being a rock star or about the rock star image. Here was a man much shorter than I was and his hair was cut in a really punk style. It was jet black with long bangs covering one eye. His skin was really smooth and his eyes were piercing through me with thick dark eyeliner. One look at the Wizard and I was instantly intimidated. This was the real deal, this was serious business! Finally, I had my chance to make it into the big time. *Hollywood, here I come.*

We were invited in. To my surprise the house wasn't really that big. It was a typical suburban home, split entry built maybe in the mid-'70s, but to me it was like a castle. As I entered I could see the living room to my left. It had twenty-foot vaulted ceilings and a mirror that covered the entire wall from the floor all the way up. The carpet was black and so plush my feet sank in it. All I was used to was old shag carpet with wild colors like lime green, orange, and red that Momma Vader bought—not because she particularly liked these colors, but these colors were the ones on clearance. And at home, it was usually taped to the floor.

We were directed downstairs to the studio, and it was like walking in a museum. I was very nervous, but I wasn't going to show it. I had always been good at staying cool under pressure and this was no exception. The studio was like the kind you would see in a commercial building. It had a long mixing console with large studio monitors built into the walls and lots of cool gadgets. There were Gold Albums on the walls, guitars, and huge tape machines. I was in awe that someone could have all of this in their home. In the back of the studio there was a drum set with a couple of amps. There wasn't much dialogue, or at least I don't remember any; we just sat down and jammed for about fifteen minutes until Prince looked at Bobby and said, "I'll take him home—you can go."

I was like, *Oh sh—! What's that all about?* I was petrified at that point. All I could think about again was what my friend Chico was telling me: "He's gonna get your booty as an initiation."

Z stood up, looked at me, and said, "Good luck." He smirked and walked away. Deep down inside I was screaming, *Please don't go!*

The Wizard asked me if I wanted anything to drink. I was thinking, *He could drug me.* I remember saying, "No, thank you," even though I was parched.

He said he was going to get dressed and would be right back. Two minutes. Five minutes. Fifteen minutes. I began to wonder, *What is this kat doing up there? It's taking a long time just to change your clothes.* Thirty minutes. Forty-five minutes and then I heard footsteps. Here he came down the stairs smelling like he just walked out of a perfume shop. Decked in black, he was ready for the night. "You ready to go?" he asked me.

Sure thing. It wasn't like I had anywhere to go with no car. We hopped into his black BMW two-door coupe and rolled out. This was no ordinary BMW. All the windows were blacked out, and I mean really black. He had custom rims that didn't appear to really fit the car. I mean, they were too wide for the car. They were at least six inches outside the wheel well and the car was really low to the ground. Inside were these black fur seat covers with all black interior. The stereo was like something out of a sci-fi movie. No sooner than we got off his property he was playing me some new music to get my reaction.

Then without hesitation, Prince just looks at me and says, "The job is yours if you want it."

He tells me to sleep on it for a couple of days. He feels I will be a good addition to the group because I am young and energetic. I am diggin' the sound. It is definitely new and innovative. I know it is gonna be a success. After about twenty minutes I am really starting to like this guy. I warm up to him very quickly and realize he is a real person underneath the Hard Rock image. He is not kinky or strange in the ways that the rumors report him to be. He drives me to my car and drops me off and tells me to let him know something by the end of the weekend. I was like, *Ummm, okay, but I can just tell you now—I'm in!*

He drives off and I am keeping my cool because I don't want him to see how I really feel. When that black BMW turns the corner people must think I just popped a molly. I am jumping up and down like a crazy man! "Yes! Yes! Yes!" I kept shouting out. I jump in my car and drive straight to the club—The Taste—to get my party on and tell all of my friends.

When I get to the club, Terry Lewis, from The Time, walks up and says, "Congratulations." *Congratulations?* I haven't told anybody yet, and I'd only left Prince's house an hour ago. How does he already know? That's when I know that I have had this job long before today's meeting with Prince. He has been watching me for a while and studying my technique and growth. I'm thinking this is why he wants me. I'm teachable and ambitious. I also pay very close attention to detail, and I guess that makes for an easy study.

PRIMPING FOR PRN

I AM NOW ENROLLED in Rock 'n' Roll University. First off, Prince mentions that I need to do some work on my appearance. I'm not quite sure what he wants me to do, though I suspect that my hair is the problem. I look in the mirror and feel unsure of myself.

One day, Prince calls to tell me that he's picking me up and taking me to a hairdresser.

Moments later, the phone rings again. "It's Prince, are you ready?"

"Yes, I'm ready . . . where are you?"

"I'm outside." I can't understand how he's calling me from outside since there's no pay phone on the block, but I run down the stairs and there he is, in his black BMW. He called me *from the car*, on a phone that tucks away in a special compartment. In 1981.

We drive to a downtown Minneapolis beauty shop. Allis, the shop owner, is a flamboyant black man. At first, I think he says his name is Alex, but it's Allis. Nearly everything that comes out of his mouth starts with "Yes, honey," and he lisps, so it comes out "Yessth, honey." I can now see where Morris Day from The Time got his character. He sounds just like him. Allis listens carefully to Prince. The two decide the Jheri curl has got to go. Allis pokes at my hair with his fingers.

"Lawd have mercy, look at these cuckabeeds."

"Can you fix this mess?" Prince implores. Allis puts his hand on his hip, studies me.

"Yes, Prin. I can cook this head up, but it's gonna take me some time." He starts to pull a comb through my hair, and the Jheri grease is building up in the teeth of it. "This is some nasty shit," he says, and starts to pull the product out of my hair. Then he brings over a bucket of white stuff; he starts working the white goop through my hair, and it is starting to get warm. He keeps pulling it through my hair, and now it's getting really hot, and then after a while my scalp feels like it's burning.

"Allis!" I yelp. "My hair is burning! Take it out!"

Prince is laughing really hard. It's so hot now. I feel like my head is going to explode. Is this some kind of joke? Just when I think I can't take it anymore, Allis puts my head in the sink and rinses cool water through my hair. He spins my chair around so I can see myself in the mirror. I am not happy: my hair is straight as a Taiwanese weave and down past my shoulders. And I look like a woman. But Prince likes what he sees. I learn very quickly I am being molded, owned, stripped of my identity for the purpose of creating a new me. Sort of a metamorphosis into a Prince variation of what he wants. Even though I don't like it, I roll with it. I am all in. How am I going to learn if I don't roll with the punches? If I don't go with the flow of this master-mind of rock image making?

I wonder what my mother is going to say.

The next morning, I get up early to catch a flight to LA with Prince and Morris. As I stumble out of my room, I'm shocked to hear my mother, who's watching me from behind her bedroom door. She shrieks like out of a horror film, "Who are you? What are you doing in my house?"

"Mom, it's me—Mark!" She has a blank stare on her face and her hands are over her mouth. She scared the daylights out of me, and my heart is slamming in my chest. Why is she screaming?

Her fear turns to tears. "My God, what have you done to your hair, boy?" I reach for my hair and remember having it done the night before. I laugh and go to look in a mirror. My head looks like I stuck my fingers in a light socket. I look like a 1970s Little Richard meets Frederick Douglass.

Eventually, Momma Vader and I both have a good laugh. She runs her fingers through my hair—it's longer than hers and neither of us has any idea what I am going to do with it. I am relieved, though, that the days of grease are over.

And I finally tell Momma Vader about the audition, and that I'm in Prince's band, and that I'm leaving this very morning for Los Angeles. She is shocked. Bewildered. She is worried for my safety. She doesn't know who Prince is. I am still her little boy, still living at home, and I am going all the way to California with a strange musician. What a nightmare for a mother. I need to reassure her.

"Mom, it's all right. Prince is a Rock Star. And this is how Rock Stars look. I'll be back in a few days."

She doesn't know how to even respond to me. She looks at me and says, "You've always been a bright young man, and I know you wouldn't do anything that you felt was flaky. Are you sure this is the path you want to take?"

"Yes, Mom. It's going to be an awesome journey. Think about it, your boy is now in a professional rock 'n' roll band."

She hugs me and tells me to get my funky behind in the bathtub. "You're not going to get anywhere smelling like that!"

# # #

It's going to be my first time on a plane. When I get to the airport, I put on my sunglasses and head into the terminal. I'm wearing torn jeans over fishnet stockings, and my crazy new hair has gotten blown every which way. I see out of the corner of my eye that people are looking at me. I'm pretty sure they're laughing at me, but I tell myself they're staring because I am somebody. I'm brimming with excitement and confidence. It is all happening for me, I think. I am unstoppable.

As I'm walking through the airport I notice people looking at me like, "What the hell just walked in?" I don't care what anyone thinks about me. I am on a journey, and I am going for the shock value of the whole thing. Call it rebellion or whatever you want, but to me it is pure liberation. I am free to be as freaky and crazy looking as I want to be. Sitting on the plane is a funny experience because I have never experienced flying. The person sitting next to me doesn't know what to make of me. He doesn't know if he should be scared or what. I am terrified throughout the flight.

I look crazy but I smell good. Prince has already gone and will meet me in California. When I land, a driver is holding a sign with my name in the terminal. It feels special. *Who's laughing now?* I wonder. I hop in a limo and the driver handles my bags and shuts the door behind me. So this is how rock stars roll? The limo has liquor in it. Real glasses with ice and snacks. This is crazy and I'm loving it. He takes me to a hotel, where there is a room reserved for me. Prince calls immediately to tell me he'll pick me up to go shopping.

Prince pulls up with Morris and they're dressed clean head to toe. They have on clothing I have never seen before. Morris is in an older-styled gangster suit with some crazy kool shoes on.

Prince looks like all his clothes are female. Very androgynous looking but still a strong masculine edge to it. While shopping, I see clothing like I've never seen in Minneapolis. I see a pair of silver shoes with red trim and I lose my mind. I got to have those silver shoes! I see shirts made out of leather-like material and silky shiny suit jackets. I am in rock 'n' roll paradise. Then we go to Melrose Avenue in Hollywood, which is lined with the coolest and most bizarre clothing stores for miles. It's a rock 'n' roll utopia! You can just walk both sides of the street all day long and never run out of interesting things to see. I buy a red-checkered suit and a leather fishnet shirt. I feel at home here.

"Let's get you a date and go hang out Hollywood-style," Prince says.

I am so wet behind the ears, I have no idea what *Hollywood-style* means. But I say "Okay," and head out into the night with my new boss and my new friend Morris.

We go to an apartment down the street and Prince knocks on the door. This absolutely beautiful girl named Ola opens it. I am hoping she's going to be my date. She is so beautiful I am goo-goo eyed and completely speechless. But we quickly realize she only has eyes for Prince. Morris looks her up and down.

"I hope she's got some friends," he whispers to me.

Ola hears him and tells us she's called a couple of her girlfriends and that they'll be right over. She grabs Prince by the shirt and pulls him into her bedroom. The door slams shut and we are left alone in the apartment. Morris looks at me and pokes his bottom lip out.

"Well, ain't this a bitch," he says. "These girls better be fine." Morris is one of the funniest guys I've ever met. His sense of humor is completely uncensored.

There's a knock on the door. Ola isn't coming out of her room, so finally Morris looks at me and pokes his bottom lip out again, then answers the door. He opens it slightly and looks out to see what they look like. He looks back over his shoulder at me. He is pouting and one eyebrow is raised as if he smells something totally grotesque. His trademark expression cracks me up whenever I've seen it.

"Hello, can I help you?"

The girls reply, "Is Ola here? Oh, you must be one of our dates."

"Oh, hell no!" he says with a high-pitched voice and slams the door shut.

I laugh hysterically. It is like watching a comedy skit on late-night television and Morris is the star. They bang on the door angrily. Ola comes running out of her room and lets her girlfriends in. They are so flippin' mad.

"He shut the door on us," they yell.

I can't stop laughing, the whole thing is just so outrageous to me.

"Prince, it's time to *go*," Morris says. He isn't having it. I am a bit perturbed by the whole blind date setup. A short time after that, I am dropped off at the hotel. No date for me. But I am fine with it—the flight and all that shopping and the long day have me worn out. I am happy to go to sleep in my hotel room. This is an exciting but very strange place to me. Besides, the hotel has plenty of excitement. I enjoy people watching and being by myself.

I don't spend much time with my boss. He checks and approves my purchases, but beyond introducing us to girls, we don't socialize much, though when we do, it's like a living comedy sketch, and Morris's trademark facial expressions, pouting, eyebrows in motion crack me up every time.

I don't know it yet, but eventually Los Angeles will become a second home to me. It's a city that lights up the night. It's full of people roaming the streets with dreams of becoming some-body. Every waiter, it seems, is an actor waiting for a break. There are fancy cars everywhere—a Lamborghini, Rolls Royce, and Ferrari all in the same day. Famous actors sit at tables at fancy restaurants that have seating extended out to the side-walks. Night clubs with VIP parking and entrance lines extend-ing down the blocks. The night air is warm and the days are hot. If the Santa Ana winds aren't blowing, the smog covers the city and there is a constant haze.

But for right now, it's time for the band to start rehearsing, and we head back to Minneapolis.

CONTROVERSY, SEXUALITY

BACK HOME FOR A FEW DAYS, we start in on band rehearsals, but the real hard-core rehearsals hadn't even started yet before I find myself back in LA for a video shoot for the new songs "Controversy" and "Sexuality." This music is very different to me. I don't understand its origin, and I don't understand the genre. It is so new, so different. It is like punk rock, but funky. I know if this music crosses over, it will pave a new inroad for black musicians around the country. It is the true definition of crossover rock 'n' roll.

When Bobby Z, keyboardist Matt Fink, and I arrive at LAX, a large white passenger van picks us up and we drive to a hotel in North Hollywood. We are right on Sunset Boulevard, in walking distance of the famous Comedy Store where people like Richard Pryor, Eddie Murphy, and John Belushi perform.

I have a few hours to kill before the video shoot, so I decide to go sightseeing. As I'm walking down Sunset Boulevard, a young black man approaches me. He knows I'm in a band by my look and asks, "What band do you play in?"

"I'm the new bass player for Prince."

He raises an eyebrow and says, "I know that band—did

they get rid of André?" He is the first of many people to ask me that question.

"I don't really know what happened between Prince and André, but I am the new bass player," I reply.

"My name is TK Carter, pleased to meet you." He goes on to tell me he's an actor. I don't really believe him because everybody's an actor in Hollywood. In the months and years to come, though, I will see him appear in several movies: *The Thing, Southern Comfort, Doctor Detroit, Runaway Train,* and many more. He's a really kool kat. I'm glad we exchanged numbers so we can stay in touch.

This is the day I get a taste of what the lifestyle of a Hollywood movie star is like. We pull up to a big studio soundstage where at the guard gate they check our credentials and we are allowed in. We drive to a select parking space and can see where there are parking spaces reserved for movie stars. I walk into the soundstage studio for the first time. It is a massive space reminiscent of an airplane hangar. It has forty-foot ceilings, cameras, large dollies, and lots of workers. Cranes everywhere, video cranes. They have a live stage built for us right in the center of this monstrosity. I must admit it is pretty unbelievable. This is a real-deal Hollywood set, and I can't even imagine what the cost of something like this is. The stage is set; this is going to be a new journey. In the beginning I thought it was the beginning—but now it's really the beginning.

"Controversy" and "Sexuality" are my first music videos. I think it's kind of odd that we are even doing videos, since we haven't even had a real band rehearsal yet.

On set, it has a very smoky feel. They blow imitation smoke all over the place. It's the beginning of the MTV era, so videos are very popular. I start to develop a whole different respect for actors. Hundreds of tedious hours, take after take. I get so frustrated starting the same thing over and over again from sunup to sundown. Take one, take two, take three. Takes for music and the choreography embedded in my brain.

# # #

Once the videos are finished we are on our way back to Minneapolis where the real rehearsals begin. Prince says, "Mark, we're going to open for the Rolling Stones. Do you know who the Rolling Stones are?"

Of course I know who the Rolling Stones are. I don't listen to their music much, but I know who they are. He is saying that our opening for the Stones is going to be a game changer. I think to myself, *I'm not too sure about that.* The Stones are known to attract a pretty rowdy audience at times. He, on the other hand, seems really excited about it. He says it's going to push us over the top. If he's right, this will be a huge break.

On the first day of rehearsal back in Minnesota, I drive way out to Bloomington where a warehouse is set up for us. It is pretty impressive: lots of big speakers and equipment I've never laid hands on before. I could definitely see the difference between the big time and the Chitlin Circuit I'm used to. I have my own technician and my own little setup: an Ampeg SVT bass amp head with an 8 x 10 cabinet, and a pedal board with distortion, flanger, and other kool gadgets. I have my own floor wedge monitors so I can hear my voice when I sing background vocals. Prince took one look at my cheap bass guitar and said, "No, give him the zebra-covered Fender Jazz bass," the same one I used in the video shoot. I'm on fire. My entire rig is on fire. It sounds so good. I'm very nervous, because this is the first time I really get to let loose with the band. The rehearsals for the video were a far cry from what we are about to get into.

Prince is looking kool as always. I come in dressed to impress. Lisa always looks at me with her sweet smirk and those sexy eyes. I can tell that she and I will become close friends. She is new in a way, too. She has only been here a year now but has learned the ropes and is very protective of me.

We started jamming on the song "Head." The sound in the rehearsal space is phenomenal to me. The bass and drums are deep and powerful in tone. Everything is wired through the PA system, so it sounds exactly like it will when we're in concert. I never realized the importance of this. I can feel every note and hear every vocal. I'm in heaven. Before we get to the first verse Prince says, "On the one," and we stop the music on the beat. We begin from the top. Sounds pretty good to me, until Prince comes up from behind me, and I feel this sharp pain going up my butt, and I'm talking about a sharp pain—he's kicked me with his high-heeled pointed boot. Hard. I am so angry I want to turn around and beat the living daylights out of him. Prince is 5′2″ and I am six feet tall. I know that one swing could put him down on the ground, but then I'd be back at 7–11 working the cash register. So I have a decision to make, and I decide to play it off as a joke and pretend that it never happened.

Then he grabs my ear and yells, "Play the bass, motherfucker!" I turn around and look at him with crazy eyes like, *What do you mean, play the bass? What does it look like I'm doing?* He comes back around again and I say to myself, *I'm gonna hurt him this time.*

This time he grabs my ear lobe really hard, pulls me to his level, and says, "You better start playing the bass, or I'll find somebody who will."

I can't understand really why he's doing this to me. I'm enraged but keep thinking about where I am. Talk about lording over a person to get your way. I feel there's no options here except to whoop his little ass! What a disaster this is, I'm going to lose my job the first day, because he just opened a can of whoop-ass and I'm about to start stomping him out! Why is he being so mean to me?

Soon I began understanding the difference between playing in a bar band and being a professional musician. As an amateur I was used to making mistakes and playing the bass softly. I didn't add a lot of dynamics to my bass playing; I would just play the song as I heard it. But I soon begin to understand what Prince was talking about. It must be a lack of feeling and approach to the music. As I begin to play harder and harder, I notice my fingers begin to blister and then bleed. It is so painful that not even Band-Aids work to relieve the pressure from the bass strings. I used to play with medium-light bass guitar strings, but after playing with Prince I would start to break the strings all the time because I would play so hard. He would never again come up to me and say "Play the bass, motherfucker," and I made sure of it.

As I leave rehearsal that day I can't stop thinking about that horrific but enlightening experience. My pride is jolted and my dignity shattered—but the anger is gone and I realize that I can get past this for the better. The next day I begin to play with heart and with as much feeling as I can conjure up until it becomes natural to me. Now I will graduate to heavy-gauge strings, so they don't break. I also noticed that playing with heavier strings makes my bass sound much deeper and gives it more of a growl, especially through the Ampeg bass rig I am playing through. I'm not used to a bass rig that large—it is pretty nice. I am used to playing with little cheap amps I would either find at garage sales or at the music store over in Northeast Minneapolis.

Also, being introduced to the Fender Jazz bass is a plus. I've never played a Fender before. I was only used to playing cheaper knock-off brands of guitars. I've inherited the zebra-covered bass amp that was André Cymone's and the zebra bass that he used to play, and all of this made a huge difference in my approach to playing in front of Prince.

Rehearsals with Prince are pretty intense. One day while laughing with the group I say, "I can't wait to come to practice tomorrow since it's Friday. . . ."

"What was that?" Prince says to me in a disturbed voice.

He turns around and looks at me and says, "Did you just say *practice*?" I'm about to find out that I've said the infamous word *practice*, which is like a death sentence in Prince's presence.

I say, "Yeah, *practice*. I can't wait to come to practice tomorrow."

"Don't ever call this practice again! We don't practice, we *rehearse*. Practice is for amateurs and you're now a professional." I think, *Wow this guy takes this stuff really seriously.* But I guess that's why he's Prince. If he's made it this far, I have a lot to learn, and I was willing and ready to learn. I remember all the countless hours I spent in the music room in high school and in people's basements and garages practicing my craft. I can only imagine that Prince must have spent triple the time I spent because he is an absolute genius at it. I have never met anyone like him.

Our rehearsal schedule varies week to week, but he does give us days off to rejuvenate, recuperate our brains. He often calls me and asks if I want to go hang out somewhere. It's a weird relationship where I can get cursed out, yelled at, or even physically assaulted and then asked to go hang out like nothing ever happened. On one particular afternoon he calls me up and says, "Hey Mark, let's go roller-skating."

I say, "You know how to roller-skate?"

"I'm good at roller-skating. Can you skate?"

"Yes, let's go to Lake Calhoun." Lake Calhoun (now known as Bde Maka Ska) is an almost-four-mile-circumference lake in the Uptown area of Minneapolis. You can roller-skate or bike or walk around the lake. It has trails for everything. You can even go fishing if you want to. I met him at the north end of the lake where everybody parks and shows off their cars—rims, paint jobs, stereo systems, etc. A lot of girls hang out there and the guys come around to show off or just hang out with clusters of different groups of people, especially if it is a nice summer afternoon. So I show up and start getting my skates on. I'm waiting for Prince to get here when I see him coming around the lake. He was already here. It is kind of funny when I see him, because he has on these leg warmers all the way up to his knees with basketball short-shorts and they are really high on his waist. They kind of look like hot pants—and they are red. It's not surprising. He always dresses out of the norm. He sits down on the bench next to me while I am sitting in the grass and putting on my skates.

I look down the path and notice this beautiful girl skating toward us. I have never seen this girl around here before, and she is absolutely beautiful! The funny thing is the look on my face when Prince sees me staring with my mouth hanging open. He starts laughing at me and says, "What are you looking at?" All I can see at a distance are her beautiful long legs and right in between her legs, Lawd! Now I have seen a lot of things, but I have never seen a girl roller-skating in what appears to be a camisole. She is getting closer and closer. It is as if she is coming right toward us! I look at Prince, grab him on the shoulder, and say, "Oh my God!! Do you see this?"

Now he's on the ground laughing so hard he's holding his stomach. I'm looking at him like, *What are you laughing at? What's so funny?* Right as she approaches us, she falls over on him and gives him a big hug! I just look and shake my head.

"You're wrong, Prince, just wrong. You knew who she was all along and you let me sit here and almost have a heart attack."

He continues in laughter and says, "Mark, meet Vanity."

Later in the week Prince tells me he is going to take her in the studio and make a girl group with her. He lets me hear "Nasty Girl," the second single for them, before there are any vocals on it. The rest will be history—Vanity 6 will soon become a sexy American pop sensation.

The Rolling Stones concert is fast approaching. Prince tells me, "If this show goes over well, we'll open for the Stones throughout their world tour and it will be a big break for us." As an outsider looking in, my first thought is, *You don't need the Rolling Stones—you're going to be huge.* I see the writing on the wall already—he hasn't seen it yet, or he just doesn't recognize it.

THRESHOLD OF A NIGHTMARE

WE ARE OPENING FOR THE ROLLING STONES, I say to myself. Only a few weeks earlier, I'd been playing a bar in Minneapolis with Fantasy, and now I am about to play the Los Angeles Coliseum in front of ninety thousand people. It's October 1981, and this will be my first real show with Prince, even though we played a practice show at Sam's a few days before—but nothing like this.

We're back in Los Angeles again, but this time it feels very different. This leg of the journey began with a wild Rolling Stones crowd: it was the first of two days opening for the Stones, and it didn't go that well for us. By the end of the opening number, we could feel that the crowd didn't respect us or our music. If today is like that, we're in big trouble.

Here we are, day two, in a stretch limo heading to the Coliseum, a scene reminiscent of gladiators being led to their execution in the Roman Colosseum for the big games.

Again, we step out on the stage.

My head is in a fog.

We open with a scathing version of the song "Bambi," off the *Dirty Mind* album, and in under a minute I get pummeled by a bag of fried chicken (by the looks of it I think it's Kentucky Fried). It hits my shoulder, then a huge pinkish-yellow grapefruit hits the neck of my bass right in the tuning keys, throwing my bass sound out of whack. I'm tuning my bass while playing, but it's so loud in the Coliseum I can't tell if I am in or out of tune. Empty bottles of Jack Daniels litter the stage, and I weave and dodge to avoid being hit as bottle after bottle is thrown from the crowd. My stage monitor sounds awful; distortion blares from the speaker. By the time we get to the pleading, bitter "When You Were Mine," one of the greatest pop songs ever played, I can't even hear my own voice in the monitors. We are dodging debris from all sides, and the crowd is so loud that their screams have become the hissing of white noise. I see an incoming grapefruit at three o'clock; it is flying in at supersonic speed and I know it's gonna be bad if it hits my face, so I turn to avoid it, and it ends up impaled on my guitar's tuning keys again. It just sticks there! *Who in the hell brings grapefruit to a rock concert?* The crowd is throwing entire bags of food at the stage.

Now women are on the shoulders of men and they're waving their hands; they're intoxicated and high and *topless*, because they've been throwing shirts and bras on the stage. Prince changes up the set on us and decides to do "Jack U Off." *This is going to be really bad,* I'm thinking to myself, *this is the '80s, guys don't jack girls off,* at least that's not the language I'm familiar with for a man playing with a woman's fancy. Maybe in the future, but not now. The crowd is going to think we're talking about homosexual acts. This may not be the crowd for such a sexual song and sure enough, when we hit the hook, "I'll jack you off," all hell breaks loose! The audience simultaneously flips us the bird and climaxes into a wild rage. I think the crowd feels like we are saying we'll jack them off, and the homophobia is becoming apparent very quickly. The final insult is when an object hits Prince upside his head. I can't tell what it is; it looks like a large silver dollar or a bottle cap. He storms off the stage, with the rest of the band hot on his heels. Now my eyes are popping out of their sockets. Oh snap, where's everybody going? I turn and run after the others like a bat out of hell!

The dream has turned into a nightmare. But it isn't over. As I remember it, Mick Jagger takes the stage and talks to the crowd. They are in a rage and start booing him. The last thing we see is a huge food fight breaking out—food and trash are flying.

Prince talks to me later that evening because he's concerned about my reaction to what I had just encountered. I can tell he's really embarrassed by it. He wanted me to experience him in all his glory with the band, but under better circumstances. "Don't worry, Mark," he reassures me. "We'll never do a gig like this again. In a few weeks we'll be playing in front of our own audience—you'll see the difference."

CONTROVERSY TOUR

WE ARE BASICALLY BACK to square one as we assemble back at the warehouse in Bloomington for rehearsals. It's not for a continued run with the Rolling Stones—this time it's our own tour. Management begins to assemble a four-month Controversy Tour and wants us ready to roll out in a month. This will be easy because we are already well-groomed and ready to hit the road.

The audience will be more of a black audience, so we put a little extra funk into the show with "Head," "Let's Work," and a funkier version of "Controversy." I'm not sure what to expect this time out because all I know is what happened at the Stones concert. I know our future is set for the big stage, but just not sure about how we're going to get there. I'm keeping my fingers crossed as the tour dates begin to surface. Our first show will be at the Stanley Theater in Pittsburgh, a city I've never visited. From there we're set to go to Washington, D.C.; Greenville, South Carolina; Baltimore; and then Charlotte, North Carolina. I'm getting excited because I've never been to any of these cities.

As we arrive in Pittsburgh, I'm more like a tourist than a musician. I make sure I choose a window seat in the van so I can look out the window at this huge city. I had read stories about the 1920s mobsters in Pittsburgh, and that era is reflected in the architecture of its tall buildings. It is a beautiful, old city. My life has changed drastically in just a matter of a few months, and now I feel I'm ready for whatever comes my way.

We arrive at our hotel and enter the lobby. In the lobby of our hotel, a pretty girl catches my eye. She is checking us out. I can tell she is wondering who I am.

"Where is André?" another girl walks up with a few of her friends and asks me.

"André doesn't play in the band anymore," I tell her. She immediately looks at me with a nasty frown and says, "What? Nah, nah, nah! So who are you?"

"My name is Mark Brown, I replaced André."

"Oh no, honey, you'll never replace André! André's *fine*." My heart sinks.

Our road manager Jamie overhears the girl. "Mark, don't pay them any mind—you'll establish your own fan base in no time," she whispers.

I keep walking, and that pretty girl is on my right. She walks up to me. In a soft, soft voice she tells me her name is Tamara. I introduce myself and shake her hand. I tell her maybe I'll see her later. I head off toward my hotel room, and when I take a quick look back at her, she looks confused—like she thinks I'm crazy to pass her up. She is pretty aggressive, and I'm not used to that. I realize how conservative Minneapolis is in comparison to the people here. "Hmm . . ."

I take the elevator to the fourth floor. The chair and bed look vintage, and the bathroom has a pedestal sink with a big white spout. The room is quiet and quite sexy. Feeling alone in a strange place, I sit on the bed, killing time before the sound check at the theater. I hear a timid knock on the door. I'm thinking it's my road manager telling me it's time to head out, but when I look through the peephole, to my surprise, it's Tamara. I don't answer, because I don't know her and I don't know what she wants. I can't understand how she knows what room I'm staying in. She knocks again.

"Mark. Mark? I know you're in there."

Finally, I open the door.

She rushes at me and grabs me by the face and presses her lips hard against mine. I am shocked.

"I want you," she says and starts to strip. Just like that, all of her clothes are on the floor.

A few hours later, Jamie wakes me up when she calls me for sound check—it's time to leave. I'm looking around the room and notice that Tamara's already gone. I'm a wreck; my hair is a mess, there's lipstick all over me, and I can smell the lingering scent of my liaison with Tamara. She has vanished. I run downstairs and jump into the van. I look in the rearview mirror and spot Tamara leaving the hotel. She is beautiful, but I am in shock.

I cannot believe what has just happened. I just had my first groupie encounter.

After the sound check, we eat dinner at the theater and then go through hair and makeup for the show. I can hear the crowd's roar from the dressing room. My stomach is knotted and twisting. Sounds become muffled in my head; it's the same feeling I had before the Stones concert.

Prince calls us to his dressing room, and we make a circle holding hands. He prays for our protection and a good show, and then says, "Amen."

It feels a bit sacrilegious to huddle in a circle and pray to God and then go out and gyrate all over the stage. It's something I'm struggling with but will have to get used to. We can hear the crowd screaming as we head toward the stage, but we can't see them. The sound from the theater is thunderous, that shrieking high-pitched white noise at high decibels. I take my position on the stage. Prince looks at me.

"Are you okay?" he asks.

"I got this."

He walks to the mic and is the consummate Rock Star. Now I see Prince in his element. He is bad to the bone. So much swag I'm in awe. He stands there with his black trench and his high-heeled boots and one leg pivoting inward. This dude is cold-blooded! He cues Bobby Z, and the kick drum hits a steady pulse at 120 beats per minute.

"Pittsburgh, are you ready?" Prince yells as the curtain rises, the noise level swells to three times what it was. Prince lets out a scream and we fall into the funk of "Controversy." The crowd goes absolutely crazy. A sea of women scream and lose their minds. I am in a long gray trench coat with white shoes. I wear black pants with white buttons running down the legs. I spin and my coat flies up in the air. I am rushing with pure adrenaline, the music is so loud and so electric, funky. I feel it in the bones beneath my skin. I spin and drop to the floor and reach out to touch a girl's hand and she passes out. They have to carry her to safety despite the fans pressed hard against the front of the stage.

Women fling bras and panties at the stage and are in a trance-like state. The crowd is singing along. They know every word: "I just can't believe all the things people say . . . Controversy."

After the show, the crowd rushes the stage and we hurry to the dressing room.

So this is what a crowd of Prince fans feels like! Prince looks me in the eyes. "You did good." His approval feels like a blessing after my rough start. My bandmates toast me. I am truly in the Land of Oz.

MOJO

AS THE TOUR PROGRESSES, I find myself in a different mindset. Every night, even though I'm doing a good job musically, I'm not feeling like I fit in. I'm the new guy and feel as if I look like the odd ball of the bunch. I have one trench coat and one pair of pants and a white shirt I wear every single night. I was never shown what to do with my hair that was completely straightened, and to make things worse Prince decided to become a barber and take a scissors to it. My clothes began to smell so bad I didn't want to wear them anymore.

The thrill of road life seemed to go from the excitement of traveling and being on a new journey to this monotonous schedule. My daily activity is easy to describe: I wake up around 7 a.m. on a tour bus as we pull into a new city around 8 or 9 in the morning. I get off the bus and check into my hotel room. I go downstairs dressed incognito because I look so different from everybody else, they would easily put two and two together. I go work out at the gym, eat, and go back to my room until it is time to go to sound check. After four months and fifty-five shows, things really do become a bit routine. Every hotel room looks the same and every city seems to have the same skyline. I quickly begin to see why so many musicians turn to drugs and alcohol—an outlet for the enormous loneliness you encounter, even though you are surrounded by so many people.

Along with this intense loneliness, I feel as if I am lost, as if my identity has taken flight. I look in the mirror and I don't recognize that person. I realize that I lost my identity the day I walked out of Allis's salon when I was there with Prince and Morris. Maybe I'm not ready for the overwhelming success that has hit me so suddenly. Depression begins crouching at the entrance of my mind as my thoughts lurk in total darkness. I have to get a grip on it, but I don't know how. I don't know why I am feeling this way. Only three months on the road and I have begun feeling like I don't fit in anymore. Maybe it's the negative energy I am getting from the Prince fans not knowing who I am and wondering why André is gone. Being told time and time again, "You'll never replace André!" by hateful female fans is very hard to swallow. It tore away at my self-esteem and I felt ugly. I guess I have thin skin. However, when I'm onstage everything is fine, because with all the excitement, fans don't stop to realize I'm a new addition to the band. They're just having fun.

♯ ♯ ♯

February 1, 1982, in Ann Arbor, Michigan, is a game changer day for me: I find my mojo. As the bus pulls into the parking lot at the hotel, I see a Walgreens and decide to go pick up some hair supplies and makeup before the show. As I am shopping, I see this really small curling iron called a 9mm micro iron. I have never seen a curling iron this small before, and it gives me an idea.

Back when I had that greasy Jheri curl, my hair was always curly, and that's what I was used to. When Prince had my hair straightened I never knew what to do with it. After three months on the road now, it looks dry and bushy. No one ever showed me how to take care of it. It was really bad when I woke up in the morning after sleeping on a feather pillow—I always had little pieces of feathers and lint stuck in my bush, and it wasn't nice at all. Even though I dressed differently, I never went out in public looking unkempt and dirty, but with my hair this out of control I was looking very messy.

When I get back to the hotel, I plug in the curling iron immediately because I only have a short time before we have to head out for the show. So I wash my hair and blow-dry it the way I normally do, and like always it is very bushy. I take the curling iron and grab a very small section of hair and curl it. I look in the mirror and laugh hysterically because it is a long Shirley Temple–like curl, but it looks pretty cool. So I keep going until I cover my entire head with these long curls.

When I finish I look in the mirror and just laugh because I look like Medusa. Had I been high and seen some eyes looking at me from the top of my head I would have turned to stone. I then become angry because I just didn't know what to do with myself. Time is running out and I have to get ready to go. So out of frustration I grab my hair with both hands and scream, roughing up my hair as if I have head lice.

But something amazing happens. When I look up again at the mirror, my hair is filled with fluffy long curls. Not Shirley Temple locks, but fluffy curls. It is no longer dry and bushy. It's shiny, long, and has totally changed my appearance. When I add the makeup it scares me half to death. I look like the guy on *The Kissing Game*. I become very apprehensive and am a little embarrassed and reserved about walking outside like this. I'm not sure what type of reaction I am going to get from people, but I already dress in a way that would eventually be called metrosexual. Now with the new hairdo and the makeup—wow! This is a little over-the-top—something straight out of the *Rocky Horror Picture Show.* I am very excited about it.

When it's time to leave for sound check, I head toward the lobby, and the reaction to this new look of mine is just what I need. I have never received this type of attention before. I feel as if I have found myself again. Image is everything in rock 'n' roll and I know that. I had a lot of learning to do, but now I feel complete. I am an entity in this band. It's time to become BrownMark.

I get in the van and the rest of the band keeps looking at me. They don't say much. They just stare at me with smirks on their faces. I bet they are saying to themselves, *Finally. Mark found his mojo.* When we arrive at the venue and head for the dressing rooms, Prince catches sight of me and starts laughing. He walks up to me and touches my hair and says, "It looks good." Phew. I thought he was going to hate it. Now that I have his approval, I am thinking maybe I can take more liberties with my image. You see, he is the boss and he pretty much dictates what we can and can't wear—even down to hair and makeup. I think he knows I am searching for an identity with him, and when I find what I'm comfortable with he lets me run with it.

The amazing thing is the fans' reactions. I didn't realize how much hair could make that much of a difference in my appearance, but it does. When I hit the stage the energy from the audience is very different for me. Maybe it's because I feel better about myself.

Our next stop is Saginaw, Michigan. I don't know what it is about Michigan, but the love for Prince and his band there is phenomenal. We had played Detroit earlier in the tour at the Joe Louis Arena and the crowd was like nothing I had ever seen before. It was ten times what it was in Pittsburgh at the Stanley Theater. Saginaw and Ann Arbor are no different. Michigan accepts me with open arms, calling me by name, even. They know I am the new guy, but that doesn't matter to them as long as I give them a good show.

We started the tour with a crowd of 2,800, typically, and by the end of the five months on the road we are playing in front of an average audience of 10,000 to 17,000 people. The LP *Controversy* is a success, just like the tour. By mid-March 1982, we play our last date in Cincinnati at the Riverfront Coliseum. There are a whole lot of people there to see us, and I know now that I am into something really big. I knew Prince was a Rock Star, but to me, with the exception of the Rolling Stones tragedy, a successful tour is the equivalent of an audience of 2,000 to 6,000 people. And to think, this is only the beginning. This album is crossing Prince over into a different genre. I wasn't around during the Dirty Mind tour, but I hear plenty about it from Bobby and Lisa. They are just as surprised as I am about the success we are having. We know it is only going to get bigger.

During sound checks in each city we have jam sessions for hours, coming up with new grooves and perfecting our sound. Some of the music we are coming up with is really good stuff, so we know the future is bright. Lisa is a brilliant pianist and has this way about her when she plays the keys. She can take a simple chord and put a twist on it that changes everything and gives it a fuller sound. Prince knows this about her, and that's why she is so valuable. Dr. Fink is named the Dr. because he is a monster surgeon when it comes to keyboard solos. Bobby Z holds a serious pocket on the drums, which makes my job as a bassist very easy. Dez is a guitarist in his own rank—he brings the rock edge to the group along with Prince's phenomenal ability to make his guitar speak. We have all developed a chemistry that we can only explain as love and respect. We really care for each other, and it shows by the way we play together. Prince loves it and gleans everything he can from it. Yes, the future is bright for this guy. He is a beast and the band he put together is a beast. Together we are a machine that is only getting stronger.

It is an exciting time for me. By spring of 1982, we are on our way home after a long six months on the road. Going back to Mom's house is a weird feeling after living in hotels for so long. I'd just turned twenty that March, and one thing was for sure, I was a different person now. I am wilder and more free-spirited than ever. Road life and traveling around the country changed my perception of life as I knew it. The country is still racially divided, but not in the way I thought it would be. My views on life were beginning to change as I experienced a more diverse America than I had previously known. Traveling was a positive experience for me—it was opening up my eyes.

Living at home after all this change was just not going to work out for me. I liked to stay out late, drink, and flirt with the girls. So I knew it was time to find my own place to live. I also wanted to purchase a nicer vehicle to fit my bad boy rock star image, but first I had to figure out what it would cost me to move away from the security of Mom's house. Since I turned eighteen she had been charging me $450 per month rent, so the way I figured, I would call up my boys and see if we could all split rent payments and get our own place. Playing in the band, I didn't make much money, but I also had no real expenses while on the road. So I was able to save up my daily per diem along with my weekly paychecks and was actually saving about $2,200 dollars a month—a lot of money to me. My bank account, for the first time, had about $14,000 in it and I was living large.

With no role models, no father figure, and no financial advice, my first thought was to buy a car. Since I had bought my first car at sixteen, I knew the process. This time I wouldn't need a co-signer: I would be paying cash. I searched the entire city looking for a new black Pontiac Firebird Trans Am. It had a new body style that looked like KITT from *Knight Rider,* from the TV series with David Hasselhoff. He had a black Trans Am that has a mind of its own. I wanted a car that looked just like that, so I searched everywhere for it, but they were sold out everywhere. I found one—a dealer down in Bloomington had the only one left in the whole state. Pontiac only made around thirty-two thousand of them, so they were scarce. I immediately hurried to the dealer and saw my car on the show floor as I drove in. They had just received it and it only had a few miles on it. Sitting in the driver's seat, checking out the interior and all the new gadgets that came with the car, I knew I was driving away with that car that day. I had been there for a while, though, and not one of the salespeople had approached me yet. Usually they're so desperate to make a sale they come running out to help, right? I figure because I am a black kid who looks too young to be able to afford this car, they are ignoring me.

So I walked up to one of the salespeople as they were all standing in a huddle laughing among themselves. "Can someone help me?"

"Help you with what?" one of the salespersons replied.

"I'm looking to purchase that Trans Am over there and I would like to test-drive it."

He looks at me and says, "You can't afford that car."

Then he turns around and walks off. I am so used to this type of behavior that it doesn't bother me. I just ask to speak to a manager.

When the manager comes up to me, he asks, "How can I help you?" I tell him I have been searching for this car all over the state and this is the only one left. He replies, "Yes, but how do you expect to pay for it? Do you have a job?"

By now I should have been belligerently spewing off obscenities, but the last laugh will be mine. So I repeat my intention to test-drive and purchase this car. He says he is too busy to take me out at this time, but that I could come back tomorrow. I say, "No, forget the test drive. I'll just purchase the car." He looks at me with a blank stare and seems to understand then that I mean business.

He then says, "I'm so sorry, but I didn't think you were serious. I thought you just wanted to drive the car—but not serious."

I'm still looking at him. "How long is this going to take? Because I'm busy."

"Well, if you don't mind me asking, how are you going to pay for it?"

"With money," I reply.

"Yes, but are you going to need a loan? Because if you do it may take a while."

I tell him I have cash and I'm ready to purchase now. He just looks at me, and I'm sure I have such a look of conquest on my face. He tells me he would be right back with the paperwork, then brings me into a private office and caters to my every need. I watch as he snaps his fingers at the turd who walked away from me and tells him to get to work writing this deal up. That salesperson looks at me in the office with this dumbfounded look on his face and starts scrambling to get the car ready along with the paperwork. When it is all said and done, they come to me with all the papers to sign, and I look at him and say, "I changed my mind."

They both look at me in disbelief. I say, "We have a deal if you give the sale to one of the other salespeople, but I will not buy anything from you that *he* gets a commission on." What a thrill it is to say this—it's one of the only times in my life I had the power to dictate what I want. I see a very nice sales lady who is helping another couple across the room, and I insist she be the one to assist me. They leave and send her over to me, and she not only takes me for a test drive—she treats me like the man I am. That feels good. I drive away with a brand spanking new Pontiac Firebird Trans Am. I have it tricked out with black tint, custom chrome rims, and a custom stereo system. I am rollin'.

# # #

Now it is time to find my own apartment. Searching for an apartment is troubling because I had never done it before. I have to contend with a known fact as well: I am black, and that is going to make it difficult. One of my buddies, Donald, was military, so that is going to be my angle to get a place. I let him deal with the landlord—for some reason that makes it easier to convince the landlord to rent to two (practically) teenagers. Donald is twenty-one and I have just turned twenty. There are four of us who are going to split the rent even though only two of us will be on the lease. Being young and inexperienced, I don't think it through that this is going to be a problem.

Within a week, we throw our first party. We have it all— loud music, liquor, drugs, and women. We party till the police come and shut us down. I also don't pay too much attention to the fact that this type of activity will make it harder for the next black tenants to be able to live in such a nice apartment complex. We get a warning from the landlord that if we have any more complaints we'll be evicted. Well, we figure we will just have another party but tone it way down, right?

Wrong. The next party we have is even bigger than the last. Word gets out that we know how to throw a party—and we throw a party! We bring in bigger speakers and more liquor. Young and dumb, that was us. We are evicted.

So it's back to Mom's house, but this time with four roommates. Things are fine at Momma Vader's house until she slaps a curfew on us. She definitely knows how to get us out. She sets the curfew to eleven at night. If we aren't home by then, we'll be sleeping on the front lawn. She isn't playing. I show up at 11:01 one night, and she has the dead bolt locked. She is on the other side of the door looking at me through the small glass window and she says, "I told you eleven o'clock. I left a blanket on the steps for you."

This isn't going to work out for me. Our other roommates are never home. They will just show up in the morning for a shower knowing they can't make curfew.

Eventually, we talk another poor soul into letting us rent her house. She is a sweet landlord and we are just foul. Too much testosterone, if you ask me. It is like the frat house in *Animal House*. I have a full band setup in the dining room, Hucky has the basement with all his DJ equipment ready to use. Robert has his weights set up in the living room, and Donald has the room connected to the attic, and Lord knows what he has going on back there. The house is constantly noisy, and we are trying hard not to have any parties, but boys will be boys. It gets to the point where we are completely out of control. The house is a revolving door for girls and musicians. It's as if we don't know what to do with our free time. We always know when Hucky is home because he drives his old beat-up Pontiac LeMans down Park Avenue going eighty, slams on his brakes, and fishtails from the other side of the street to his parking space in front of the house. His doors don't open so he uses the window to climb in and out of his car. There is smoke from the burning rubber and his stereo is blasting so loud it's distorted. Hucky often jumps out with a six-pack, and the whole neighborhood knows he is home. I am often in the dining room with a bunch of musicians jamming full volume. And the whole house smells like weed. All the time. The neighbors hate us.

It isn't long before we are back at it again, despite the threat of eviction. This time we decide to throw the party of all parties. We have seven kegs in the backyard, live entertainment on the main level, a DJ in the basement, and gambling and whatever else in the attic. We have so many people that their cars are double-parked for four blocks. It's so loud. We all know this is it—eviction for sure—so we might as well have a blast. Around two in the morning, the neighbors have had enough and call the cops.

The next morning we assess the damage, and it is not good. The cabinet doors are hanging by the hinges in the kitchen, and the hardwood floors are filthy. There is trash everywhere from the front yard to the back alley. And to make it worse, the landlord just happens to show up on an unscheduled visit. We are doomed. It's back to Mom's house for me, but my roommates have to find their own place this time. Momma V is not having it.

1999

WE WORK ON THE 1999 ALBUM at Prince's home and studio in the spring of 1982. The rehearsals before we go back on the road are brutal but interesting, because it's a truly creative collaboration. We jam from morning until late afternoon, day after day, working on the same songs nonstop. I play my bass with a wireless pack so I can move around and not miss a lick. Since we're often not given any time to take breaks, I learn to play one-handed while I am in the restroom. When I get hungry, I make a sandwich with one hand on the neck of the bass, while the other hand maneuvers the knife, bread, cheese, and Miracle Whip. As we get closer to starting the tour, rehearsals go until ten at night.

Sometimes Prince gets an idea for a song in the predawn hours of the morning and wants us all to get into the studio, right then and there. I have a "bat phone," and nobody but Prince has the number, so when it rings at three in the morning, I know it's him. I learn the hard way that if I don't answer it, he sends someone over to my house to pick me up. If I'm not home to get the call, I get an earful the next day about why I wasn't at the studio when he wanted me there. It makes me a little crazy, but I focus on the money I'm earning, and I love being a musician. My pay has been increased to $425 a week, which for me is a lot of money.

I know this hard work will raise my game.

It's also time to get some new show wardrobe; my dusty gray trench coat is officially retired, and Prince wants us to have a flashier look. I go with him to pay Louis Wells and Vaughn Terry a visit, Prince's designers who are fond of big-shoulder designs, which will be interesting because I already have really wide shoulders. I look through different fabrics and find a shiny purple material that floats my boat.

I say, "I want this one!" Prince looks it over.

"Are you sure you want this? Pick another one because you'll need a backup."

I pick a less-flashy lavender fabric that still has some snap-crackle-funk. Dry cleaning on the road is an issue, so having a few options for wardrobe is important. I have pants made from the fabrics I've selected, with big buttons going down the legs.

Not only does my wardrobe get revamped, but I also retire my zebra-striped Fender Jazz bass for a custom purple Jazz bass from Fender. Our entire show has expanded and enlarged from one semitruck and three tour buses for the band, crew, and show members, to two semitrucks and six buses. We have an enormous sound system, tons of lights, set pieces, and lots of wardrobe. We're going to be playing in massive venues this time out, which requires us to bring a lot of our own sound and light gear. Everything is amped up and ramped up, and it's an exciting time. The show will be spectacular in scale and show-manship.

We have dress rehearsals on our custom stage and run the entire show as if we're performing for an audience. Prince has the rehearsals videotaped for us to study and improve the show. At our first dress rehearsal, I strut out of my dressing room in my shiny bright purple custom-made trench coat and matching pants. I have white shoes and a purple bass—I feel like a million bucks.

Until Prince lays eyes on me. "You can't wear that."

Just like that.

"It's too shiny—you're dressed like me, and this is my show, Mark," he snaps.

I go back to the dressing room where I sit and sulk. I reluctantly put on the lavender suit. He doesn't like this either—but now it's all I have. And it is going to have to last me for months on the tour.

We have a vigorous rehearsal, and during the drum and bass breakdown in the song "Delirious" I am choreographed to run, drop onto my knees, and slide to the edge of the stage into a bass break. I slide, but my satin pants don't. They rip from the knees down to my ankles—my kneecaps are bleeding—and most embarrassing of all, the crotch has ripped out of the pants and all of my junk is hanging out. The pants need emergency alteration on the knees so they won't tear out and they add a gusset made of stretchy material in the crotch. Until these repairs are made, I wear the flashy trench for a few shows. The moment the pants are fixed, it's back to the boring wardrobe. I try to focus on the fact that I have a job I love, a nest egg in the bank, and a sweet ride.

I have no cause to complain. Life is good.

The 1999 Tour has a very short first run. Whenever a band starts to get really successful, it's not unusual for problems to arise. Dez and Prince aren't seeing eye to eye, and it's clear that Dez is disgruntled by the incredibly long sound checks. He is having a moral conflict with some of the music, and he's eager to move on with his own career plans. Prince also is having problems with women. His new status as a famous rock star means that Vanity is vying, along with several other lovely women, for his time and attention. They all want to be on his arm and in his bed. He has his own tour bus, and I can only imagine the drama going on in there.

The audience is also changing. Our opening act, The Time, is a funky force to be reckoned with—and they hold a lot of appeal for our black audience. Prince's music is crossing over, though, and our show is catering to more of a white audience as well. The Time gains more and more audience favor with every show, and the predominantly black audience that has been attending and supporting our concerts all this time isn't finding Prince as fresh and funky as they remember.

Prince and The Time are clashing, too. Our lineup is Vanity 6, for the preshow, with The Time playing behind a screen before they take center stage to open for us. I hear rumors that The Time is disgruntled by the fact that their pay structure doesn't change when moving from playing backup to Vanity 6 to playing as opening act for Prince.

The drama is too much, and Prince takes us off the road for a few weeks to revamp the show, revise the set, and fix personnel issues. It's a good decision. When we get back on the road, we have a show that is a masterpiece of funk jams, incorporating pop and rock elements. Part of the tweaking includes sending The Time off to do their own tour. It's just my opinion, but I think Prince sees them as a distraction and competition; it is time for them to have their own tour too. They need to be set free to see if they can fly with their own set of wings.

Starting off the second leg of the tour in Florida, I experience wings of another kind. It is a late February evening in Tallahas-

At my grandma's house in south Minneapolis around 1969: When I was older, I could walk around the corner to a music store on Lake Street.

My school photo in ninth grade.

Talent show at Washburn High School. Joe Scott (*right*) and I are on guitar and Harlan "Hucky" Austin (who would later become Prince's bodyguard) is on vocals.

At the Fox Trap in Minneapolis with Fantasy around 1977. Photograph by Charles Chamblis. Courtesy of Minnesota Historical Society.

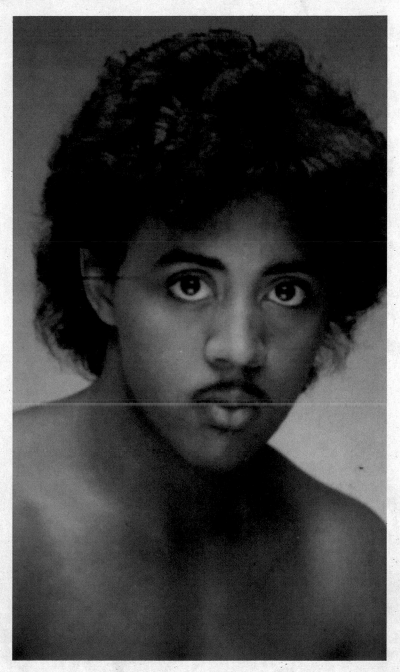
A new publicity photo in 1981. Photograph by Allen Beaulieu.

The infamous concert opening for the Rolling Stones in Los Angeles, October 1981. Photograph by Allen Beaulieu.

(*above*) With Prince and Dez at the Met Center, March 7, 1982.
Photograph by David Brewster/Star Tribune/Getty Images.
(*below*) This promo shot for *Purple Rain* is when I first started
wearing the headscarf, and I've been wearing one ever since. Prince
pulled one end down over my eye. Photograph by Nancy Bundt.

10-18-84

On the road during the Purple Rain Tour. These photographs were taken by Karen Krattinger, one of my favorite staff with Prince and The Revolution.

(*above*) Just waking up on tour. My friend Scott Bogen took this shot—I don't even remember him in my room to get this photo. (*below*) Promo photo for the Purple Rain Tour, taken in the bleachers at a venue before a concert in Atlanta. Photograph by Nancy Bundt.

 BROWNMARK

(*above*) Life with Motown, circa 1987. (*below*) The road goes on. With The Revolution at First Avenue in Minneapolis in September 2016. Photograph by Lisa Jarema.

see. I'm sitting in my hotcl room when I peep something skittling across the floor. It is a two-inch-long, fat cockroach. It's huge and it's disgusting. I grab the *Yellow Pages*, three inches thick and heavy, and chuck the book at the behemoth beast. It bashes the bug with an explosive bang. I am so creeped out by this bug from hell that I jump off the bed and stomp on the *Yellow Pages*. I go back to bed, feeling victorious. When I wake up the next morning, the *Yellow Pages* book is where I left it. But the bug is gone. *What the hell?* I'd heard him crunch! I'd jumped on the book!! I then learn these freaks of insect nature are the larger, well-armored relatives in the roach family, and they have wings.

Early in the tour schedule, guitarist Jesse Johnson from The Time and I have another frightening experience. It is a cold December day in Detroit, and we are bored just sitting around in our hotel rooms, so we have the limo driver take us to the nearby mall.

"We'll be back in an hour," we say and head to the shopping center. It appears we stand out a bit at the mall, with our funky hairstyles and funkier clothes. I notice as we pass by people that they are staring at us. I glance quickly over my shoulder and am shocked by what I see.

"Whatever you do, don't turn around," I whisper to Jesse.

"Why?" he asks.

"There are about 150 girls following us."

Jesse turns around anyway.

We duck into a candy shop to talk to a manager. The girls behind the counter recognize us. The manager comes out from the back of the store. The crowd is starting to push in, and we are sure we're gonna be two dead, smashed roaches.

"What the hell is this?" he asks when he sees the crowd behind us. We tell him who we are and what appears to be happening, so he calls mall security. But we're afraid they won't arrive in time. This is feeling like it could turn into something bad. We ask if there is a back door into the alley behind the store and contact the limo driver to meet us there. We start to leave and turn to look one last time at the mob.

It's a terrible mistake.

"It's them! I told you it was them!" a girl yells, confirming for the others. They all start screaming and the crowd quickly swells, a giant wave of girls, pressing in to crush us, and we are forced to jump over the counter to make our getaway out the back door. The driver isn't there yet, and we wait, praying the crowd doesn't come pouring through the door into the alley. *I swear, I will never go out by myself again,* I say to myself.

But soon enough, in Boston, Dez and I get bold and decide we're going to head out to a club on our own. We don't tell our security, because we don't want them tagging along and cramping our style. We tell our driver to meet us with the car in five minutes outside the hotel. When Dez and I meet in the lobby, we look out the window and see three hundred excited fans waiting to greet us, held at bay by a police barricade across the street.

"We love you!" female fans scream. Our limousine is at the curb. All we have to do is run really, really fast down the steps and get in the limo before the crowd realizes what's happening. Dez and I tear like maniacs down the stairs and arrive at the car. We got this!

The limo's doors are locked. And the driver is not inside.

Like a siren going off, the air fills with the piercing screams of hundreds of fans about to storm. If the Detroit mall girls were a tsunami, this is a category-five hurricane brewing. We know we won't make it back up the stairs without being swept up.

We are *so* doomed.

"Let's brace ourselves around this pillar," Dez yells, and we grab on to it for dear life just as unrestrained fans touch down and swirl around us. Hands tear at my hair and grab at my clothes, trying to rip my shirt and my pants off of me, and their hands are all over my body, and they are grabbing at *everything,* sexually groping me, and I'm so grateful my clothes are leather so they don't rip. We're holding on tight, hoping to not get pulled from the pillars. Just then, the security team rushes into the crowd, grabs us, and pulls us to safety inside the hotel. Turns out, the driver was at the bar enjoying a cocktail, completely unaware.

On the tour, I wake up early mornings to work out with Big Chick, Prince's personal bodyguard. Big Chick is a huge white guy; his arms are bigger than my thighs, and he can bench-press 450 pounds-—and that's just a warm-up. He is one tough dude. He and I become close friends. One morning in Alabama, we walk a block to the local gym that's available to hotel guests. When we walk in, the men there become completely silent and stare at us. I feel like I've walked into a Klan meeting. They clearly are not happy to see a black man on the premises.

Chick knows about these types of people and gives them a verbal warning.

"This is my friend and if you little pussies have a problem with him, then you have a problem with me," he says. They continue to stare angrily. Now Big Chick is angry. He yells, "Whatchoo mitches lookin' at? You ain't gonna do nothin'." The entire gym clears out. They can't abide working out with a black man in their gym. And they sure don't want to experience the wrath of Big Chick.

Another morning, I am two minutes late for the slated departure time of our tour bus, and Prince tells the driver to leave. When I come down to the lobby with my bags, the bus is gone! It's just me—and a bunch of fans asking for my autograph and laughing at the same time, teasing me about the fact that they've left me behind. What is annoying is that we sometimes have to wait on the bus more than an hour after the departure time for *him,* but he waits for no one.

I find a pay phone and call my mom to tell her what's happened.

"Come home, son—that is uncalled for," she says. I call for a taxi to take me to the airport.

The power trips on this tour are really wearing me out. Prince is falling out with everybody. Most of the time he's pretty cool with me, but then for no reason he just flips out. When he acts up, it's like I don't even know him. I do my best to remain professional and not take his attacks personally. I sense my days are numbered. I have been preparing to leave.

"The bus is coming back!" I hear a few fans yell.

I don't make a move to get on the bus. Prince sends Big Chick out to talk to me. He tells me he knows that what Prince did was messed up. I tell him I am so mad I might hurt him if I see him. Eventually, Big Chick talks me into getting back on the bus. I don't even look at Prince when I get on. I go to bed without a word to him and don't wake until we get to the next city. I wonder why he is on our bus in the first place—he has his own bus.

At the Rockford Metro Centre, it feels like everything is flowing. We are jamming on the ballad "Do Me Baby" and midway through the song we always break it down while Prince entertains the audience with his sexual dancing and what-not. To my shock and horror, a large banner with the words WE LOVE YOU, BROWNMARK stretches across a section of the audience.

Prince stops the show.

He points me out. "Do you think he's fine?" he yells. The crowd cheers. "Wait a minute. I said, DO YOU THINK HE'S FINE?"

The audience ramps it up, cheering me on.

He turns his butt to the audience and shakes it, yelling, "But does he have an ass like mine?!!"

I feel deflated.

What could be my hard-won moment in the sun turns into a pissing contest, one that continues for the rest of the tour and for a long time after. I have zero interest in this contest. I have no desire to compete with him. That would be like racing my Trans Am against his Ferrari. I don't want to be a superstar. I just want to play my bass and have fun and make music that makes people feel good.

After that incident, I am frequently the target of Prince's blasts and attitude. I certainly am not the only one, but it starts to feel as though he is out to get me, because people are responding to my performance. He needs all the attention to be on him.

I am relieved when the tour finally ends in April 1983. Five months is a long time to be on the road. I am motivated to push forward with my own agenda: getting my own band Mazarati into the studio to record our first album. It's looking like it might be time for me to break free and find my own way.

Prince, it seems, has been eager to get through this tour too. He's been preoccupied with developing his next project, a little film about a guy trying to make it in the music industry.

He's calling it *Purple Rain*.

THE SHADOW

HOME FOR THE SPRING, and I have lots to accomplish. First, I need to get out of my mom's house and find my own place—again. I have been paying her a little bit of rent every month, even when out on the road, and I've saved up some money. I am young to be thinking about purchasing a house, but I want to give it a try anyway. I find a realtor and the search is on. I am looking outside the Twin Cities for a house where I can find needed solitude, peace, and quiet.

I feel like my days with Prince are coming to an end. His behavior toward me has shifted. I am incredibly grateful for the training he has given me; I know I might still be playing in a garage band on the Chitlin Circuit if it weren't for him showing me the ropes and bringing me into his band. It seems like he wants to keep me small and in the shadow, and I want to stretch and grow. I know it will be quite an undertaking to put the band Mazarati together. I secure a management team for them because I don't want to reveal that I am the person behind their development. I wear disguises, such as a gold mask, to the shows because I don't want Prince to know that I am preparing to branch off on my own. The band calls me The Shadow and I finance Mazarati's productions to get them launched. I have learned from Prince how to organize and prepare a band for performance. We work from sunup to sundown in my mom's basement. The guys work incredibly hard; they are hungry for success and tell Momma Vader they will follow her House Mother Rules: no drugs, no alcohol, and no girls. Well, that's what they say they are going to do. But these guys are party animals. After a month of reports from the neighbors, and my mom returning home night after night to find girls and worse in her house, the time comes for Mazarati to go. We begin to rehearse in an old warehouse that belongs to the Klein family, owners of Klein Chevrolet in the Uptown neighborhood of Minneapolis.

I showcase the band at a local club, the Cabooze, and it is a sold-out show. This is a phenomenal start for a new band just coming out of a basement or a warehouse. Every month throughout the summer, their popularity grows. I know I'm on to something special with this band.

I work days with Prince and the band, and nights with Mazarati. I create original material for them, developing a unique sound that won't link them with other bands in the area. The Minneapolis musical scene is on fire and record company reps are scouting talent nonstop, looking for the next big breakout band. Mazarati's star is rising.

There are big changes to Prince's band around the same time. He'd always had it in mind to separate himself from the band, and he eventually seals it by giving us our own name: The Revolution. Dez leaves, as I suspected he would. He starts his solo project, moving in a different musical direction. Lisa's partner in crime, Wendy, who had traveled with us off and on through the 1999 tour, is a good guitar player. Prince asks my opinion about adding her to the band in the rhythm guitar spot, and I think she'll be good. She's talented, young, and hungry. She's younger than I am, so I won't be the kid in the band anymore, which is also a bonus. I agree to get her up to speed with the choreography and stage presence, and Prince works with her on refining her guitar skills.

Just when I think my plate couldn't get any fuller, Prince wants to work on a soundtrack for the *Purple Rain* movie script he's developed. We all think he's a little crazy. But he's shown me more than once that he possesses a kind of genius instinct—and I don't doubt that he'll make this work. As it turns out, there's a part for me in the film. He gives us all scripts and immediately signs us up for acting classes.

I am now not only developing and recording my own band's music, but also working on a soundtrack, taking acting classes, and the search is still ongoing for a house. At long last, my realtor finds a property that fits, and we drive to Eden Prairie, twenty minutes southwest of Minneapolis. Hidden behind a hill of sumac trees, up a steep driveway, I see a dark-brown cedar house set far back on nearly an acre of land with a perfectly manicured yard. I fall in love with the full basement—it would be for my recording studio. It is costing three to four thousand dollars per song in recording fees for Mazarati, and I want at least twenty-five songs for our album. That means a cost of $100,000 out of my pocket for the album. I go ahead and build the studio for $75,000 and work and record everything there.

I am twenty-one and rollin' in the dough. I own a house with a recording studio, a sports car, and after the success of the song, I buy my own little red Corvette, a 1972 Stingray. She's a real beauty. I even buy a boat. I have no guidance with money; I just know I want everything money can buy. I do figure out that if I want to carry on this lifestyle, I will have to be successful in the execution of all these projects. There is a long road of hard work ahead of me.

# # #

One night, I am rolling around south Minneapolis in my Corvette, looking for a party. At one of them, I run into this girl I have always thought was on fire. Her name is Angelique. We're both bored at the party, so I offer to take her home. I am pretty sure we both have the kind of ulterior motives the very young and hormonal have. We're tooling down the highway talking about nothing when suddenly the car starts spinning out of control and slams into a railing. The car explodes into fiberglass pieces with the impact. I see the hood of the car hurtling toward me. Then there is another boom, and my car is now on top of the guardrail.

This is it. The car is going into the Mississippi and I'm going to die, I think, just before blacking out.

I regain consciousness when Angelique slaps my face hard to keep me from going into shock. I open my eyes and I am lying on the asphalt of Highway 494. Out of the corner of my eye, I spot another mangled car on the road. Two ambulances, sirens screaming, arrive on the scene, one for me and one for the other driver. The smell of gasoline is all around me. I hear the police on the scene tell the ambulance driver that the other accident victim is a woman in bad shape who had been drinking. My leg is throbbing and my face is burning. The pain pushes me into unconsciousness.

I'm grateful to see another day. I learn that a woman driving at a high rate of speed struck my car, and that's what put my head through the windshield.

A few days later, even though I am on crutches, I go to my wrecked car to retrieve my belongings. There is virtually nothing left. The rims are bent in half, the windshield is blown out, and all the fiberglass body has shattered. The battery exploded, which explains all the tears on my skin. With the impact my kneecap had been jammed into my thigh bone, and I have a concussion from the crash into the windshield. I had been bleeding and the pain was pushing me toward going into shock. Thankfully, Angelique had been wearing her seatbelt (I wasn't) and so she came out without a scratch. Despite their fiberglass bodies, I still love Corvettes.

A few days later, I buy the latest model of the Corvette; she's sturdier with big back tires. When I drive up to the studio in my new car, ready to work, Prince looks at me like I'm crazy. "You almost killed yourself, and you go buy another one?"

It hasn't entirely sunk in that I've been in a serious accident and could have lost my life. When I hear his words and see the look on his face, I grasp the fact that I had come frighteningly close to losing everything I've worked so hard to build.

♯ ♯ ♯

We start working on the *Purple Rain* soundtrack. We go to acting classes early mornings and rehearse all afternoon. Acting classes are quite the experience, and I gain a real appreciation for what actors do. They make it look so easy. My favorite part of the classes is doing improvisational scenes. We go over the songs "Purple Rain" and "Let's Go Crazy" for hours upon hours.

One of the scenes proves really awkward for me. I have to do a scene with Susan from Vanity 6, and the circumstances require that we demonstrate that we are a married couple and intimate with each other . . . in front of everyone. Knowing that she is one of Prince's ladies makes me really nervous. But acting teaches me to let go of my inhibitions. It really takes me out of my comfort zone and unleashes emotions and an inner life I didn't even know were inside me.

By the time we begin filming, my injuries from the accident are healed, but I am in for another kind of hurt.

For weeks I rehearse my lines for the movie. When *Purple Rain* filming starts, I am really prepared for my part, and I just know I'm gonna kill it in front of the camera. I arrive to the set, full of anticipation for this crucial turning point in my career. After all, this is going to be my opportunity to make my mark in Hollywood, right? Wrong.

A producer tells me that all of my lines are cut.

I am required to be on the set every day for two weeks of shooting, and I don't have any lines. At all. Nobody tells me why. It appears I am the mute band member. During all this time, the director never speaks a single word to me. It's as if I am invisible.

Eventually, Prince explains the situation.

"Mark, we had to cut the film down because it was too long." He is very matter-of-fact and unapologetic. "That's why we cut your parts out."

Emotionally, I am feeling let down. But on the upside, I figure I'm getting paid for doing nothing. I spend most of my time on the set at First Avenue nightclub just walking around, watching and learning about moviemaking. I am able to get a glimpse of Prince acting in some of the scenes, but mostly it is a closed set; nobody can be on set when he is acting. Prince is in total control of everything around him. The dailies are fun to watch because I can see what the scenes look like at the end of each day of filming. It's weird seeing the acting scenes performed without any music to set the mood. Just people acting out their parts, and it's clear that nobody in this film is a well-trained or capable actor.

I hear the word *cut* a million times. Maybe two million.

Prince is the happiest I've ever seen him. He is living his

dream; he has started from nothing and has worked his way up to writing and acting in his own movie. He toils tirelessly day and night on the film. The musical performance scenes are nothing new to any of us in the band. They're exactly like all of the demanding rehearsals we have before a gig. We do take after take after take: it feels like a glorified music video, so I am used to the long hours under the hot lights. I have one scene where I look at my watch as if I'm mad because everyone is late for rehearsal. It is shot during the "Computer Blue" sequence. This acting bit helps somewhat to take the sting out of the situation. Somewhat.

I have spent money to join the Screen Actors Guild, taken hours of acting classes, and signed off on all the actor talent contracts, only to have my heart and ego smashed. But I am also not completely surprised. On a regular basis, I have been silenced before I can speak in this new endeavor of Prince's, and his focus with this project is entirely on the young women. They have become the centerpiece to his vision for the movie.

I fall into a depressed funk; I'd expected the movie to shine a bright light on my talent. I'd worked hard at my lines. I envisioned success as an actor and a musician. I try to keep reminding myself of all the great projects I have going on. I try to focus on the things I can control, but I find myself turning to alcohol as a way to escape the negative feelings surrounding all that is out of my control. I am overwhelmed with anger and sorrow. I feel oppressed as part of the machine that The Revolution has become without recognition for all the creative input I tirelessly added to the success of what we are accomplishing. I fall into a pattern of self-destructive behavior. Whenever Prince leaves town for weeks at a time, I go to First Avenue on Thursday nights and party until the bar closes. Then I throw an after-party at my house in Eden Prairie. The house is packed with twenty-five to fifty people who stay and party with me until Sunday morning. This goes on for some time. My loneliness, depression, and anger turn me into the sex, drugs, and rock 'n' roll stereotype I told myself I would never become.

During this time, I'm approached by Rick James, Miles Davis, and others who invite me to play on tours with them. They offer triple what I am paid working with Prince and The Revolution. I decline, time after time, because Prince keeps telling me, "Stick with me and the band, and you'll never have to work another day in your life. Think about it; we're doing a movie and a world tour. I'm going to cut you guys in on the money this time." This is an appealing carrot to dangle in the face of a twenty-two-year-old.

But the truth is that I am now literally being kept in the dark: my position onstage is not well-lit. It feels like I am slowly being phased out. I am not included in interviews with the band, and nobody tells me why. I am in an awkward position but choose to stick with Prince and continue to hope that staying with Prince and The Revolution will pay off.

The movie is edited and ready to be screened. I opt to just wait to see it when it premieres in Hollywood. I'm a poor sport about everything related to the film, because I'm so humiliated with having been rendered silent in it. I don't go to the private local screenings—I don't want salt rubbed in my wounds.

♯ ♯ ♯

When we arrive in Los Angeles, we discover that the premiere is ramping up into a really big deal—much to our surprise. None of us expected this film to amount to anything. We're all just happy we got it done. We discover the plans include a screening at Mann's Chinese Theater in Hollywood, with the classic red-carpet rollout. We learn that the press, film executives, and big stars are planning to attend. Since we arrive several days before the premiere, we have some much-needed rest and relaxation time. My buddy Harlan (aka Hucky) Austin and I intend to take full advantage of this. Hucky has been my friend since we were both nine years old. He is working as Prince's bodyguard, and during downtime we like to hang out together. We both drive Ferraris; his is burgundy. I drive a red 308 GTB. We love to roam through Beverly Hills. What a sight we are—two young black men driving $100,000 cars in one of the most affluent cities in the country.

One day, after aborting what I realize is a reckless race through Laurel Canyon at ridiculous speeds—the lesson of my little red Corvette momentarily forgotten—I suggest we hit Larry Parker's Diner, a 1950s-style Beverly Hills hotspot famous for Haagen-Dazs milk shakes and telephones in the booths.

We sit down and immediately peep two gorgeous ladies in a booth across the room. There is just one small problem—they are with dates. I call and ask our mutual friend Lance to call from an outside line to their booth. When the phone in their booth rings, they all look at it like it's evil or possessed. Finally, one of the girls tentatively picks it up. "H-hello?" Lance tells her, "The two guys across the way are interested in you ladies. You should dump the guys you're with." The young woman laughs out loud. One of them comes over and says we get points for originality. But they both decline the invitation to join us.

At the end of the night, though, when the girls see us leaving and see the cars we're getting into, they promptly ditch their dates. We're now worthy of their attention, it seems. We hop into our cars, squealing out of the lot with a tire-peeling roar. Hucky and I are both grinning from ear to ear. The look on the girls' faces as we drive off into the Hollywood night, leaving them standing in the parking lot, is priceless.

On July 27, 1984, the morning of the *Purple Rain* premiere, I turn on the television and see the news channels broadcasting announcements about the film's screening at Mann's Chinese Theater. They report that Hollywood's elite in attendance will see what the up-and-coming pop star has conjured for the big screen. It is promising to be a star-studded event, and I don't even know if the movie is any good.

Can it get bigger than this? I ask myself as we step out of the limousine and walk the red carpet that leads to the theater. Cameras click nonstop. The crowd screams from behind barricades. I see really famous musicians on the carpet. Once inside Mann's, we are escorted to a special section of the theater. I look around the audience and see movie stars and big directors. Finally, it's time for the film to start.

The lights in the house begin to go down. I'm worried. What if it's really bad?

I know Prince has big plans for the future, promising plans for all of us. He wants to build a huge complex where we'll produce bands, movies, soundtracks, and have personal control of all sorts of projects. He wants to call it Paisley Park. Prince has plans to become King, and I'm still somehow excited to be a part of it. But if this film doesn't go well, that dream may come crashing down. I am nervous. As the movie plays, I am not at all happy. I think it's pretty bad, and I'm feeling disappointed. If I were a movie critic, I'd give it a C at best.

The credits start to roll at the end of the film and to my complete shock, the crowd applauds and there is an outcry of joyful cheering. Prince and all of us are looking at each other in complete surprise—none of us, not even Prince himself, anticipated this outrageous response. The crowd cheers and yells and hollers nonstop as our entourage leaves the theater. Getting into the limo, I hear fans screaming, "We love you, Brown-Mark!" I am feeling the love too.

Somehow, we have won the lottery for the third year in a row—and I'm ready for the payout.

LET'S GO CRAZY

THE PURPLE RAIN ALBUM is a huge hit, and the time comes again to tour and promote the album. The shows sell out instantly. The production for the tour is gargantuan, with a costly convoy of approximately twenty-five trucks and buses to move all the crew, and a legion of semitrucks to transport the equipment. I'm staying in five-star hotels and flying in private jets. We've got bodyguards, personal chefs, top-shelf booze, and beautiful women. I have high hopes of fattening my skinny wallet. I might be qualifying for higher credit these days, but that's different from real money. This tour is going to be different because we're promised a percentage of profits from the sale of merchandise: clothing, books, and posters—a new development that will make all my hard work and staying the course finally pay off.

The tour is a beast. Our first leg of the concert is in Detroit, with seven nights at the Joe Louis Auditorium. The tour goes from November 4, 1984, to April 7, 1985, and we play almost every night. When we're not playing, we're traveling. It is so grueling that we have to get B-12 shots to help keep up our energy. Our bus drivers have guns, which makes me nervous. Even the bodyguards start carrying heat because cocaine, rock 'n' roll, and groupies are a dangerous combination, and things seem always on the verge of going out of control. I'm not sure Prince or any of the other band members notice, because I'm pretty much the only guy who spends time hanging out with the roadies, bodyguards, and drivers. It sounds odd, but I get the feeling that Prince's head is already on to something else. For the concerts, the costumes and wardrobe styling are reminiscent of the eighteenth century, with ruffled shirts, brocade coats, and feathers. The shows are inspired of course by the *Purple Rain* movie soundtrack, and those are the songs we're playing for sold-out houses.

Our sound checks are a different story. We're creating music that smacks of Prince's new obsession: the Beatles. On this tour, we use sound checks like jam sessions, and frequently as recording sessions. A semitruck houses a full recording studio, and it travels all over the country with us. Every afternoon at around 3:30 we are called to the stage for a sound check, but we use this time to work on and record new music for the next album. We work on fresh grooves right up until the doors open for the show. I don't mind working this hard because I know this is securing our future. This means there will be no lapse between *Purple Rain* and our next LP. We are creating an original sound, and we know this effort will birth music for the next big hit. Prince is tireless when it comes to writing music and working, and he expects us to be too, even when I'm dog-sick with a 101 degree temperature. We work in spite of being ill because we're all expected to be onstage at sound check before the show to work. Every time we meet, Prince has different songs he's created in a studio. I don't think he ever sleeps. It's during this time that we perfect this new sound for the *Around the World in a Day* album.

The Purple Rain shows are transforming every week. People jam onstage with us. Prince invites Sheila E's band, or

Apollonia 6, to join us. Bruce Springsteen and Madonna jam with us. Even random audience members are invited to dance onstage during the song "Baby I'm a Star." Eventually, Sheila E becomes our opening act and plays along with our encores. The stage is a party and we're having a blast playing, but it's also problematic. We rely on Prince's hand signals to cue us, but they're hard to follow with so many people onstage, and things are chaotic. He insists we listen and watch him to lead us at all times. "Hit me two times" is an easy instruction to follow, but when he yells, "Hit me twenty-five times," we have to do a percussive hit twenty-five times, and if we miss one, we are fined a hundred dollars.

We're making decent money, and I suspect we may actually be the hardest-working band in show biz. Not only are we performing our shows, but we're also simultaneously creating our next album.

♯ ♯ ♯

On the road, we discover the whole country has caught purple panty fever. The ladies are especially sick with it, and one night I am the target of a frenzied fan's obsession. I step off the hotel's elevator and head to my room after a concert. It has been prearranged that this floor is blocked by security so nobody can enter unless they are part of the entourage. As I round the corner toward my room, I hear the fire escape door slamming shut behind me. I find it odd, but I know the security team does regular sweeps, so I don't worry about it. I hustle into my room, because I have only fifteen minutes before taking off to our next city on the tour bus, and I have to pack my bags. There's a knock on the door, and it's the luggage handlers, and I hand off my bags. A moment later, there is another knock. Thinking that the handlers have forgotten something, I open the door without first looking through the peephole.

Never a good idea.

Standing there is a girl in a teal-colored see-through lace top and a silver satin micro-skirt. She locks eyes on me and starts to breathe heavily. Her eyes are enormous and glassy and her face is flushed. I look down the hall for someone from the security team.

How in the world did this girl figure out where we were staying? There are code names for all of us.

She lunges, pushing me back into the room, and throws her arms around me, trying to kiss me. I gently push her away. This is awkward and I don't want to be mean, but she has to go.

"Whoa, I don't even know you," I chuckle, trying to keep it light.

But she is dead serious. "I love you so much, I want you to make love to me right now!"

I am shocked and before I can respond, she's dropped her skirt and thrown off her top and stands there, naked. I bolt out of the hotel room. I don't see any of the security detail. I tear off to the elevators and she streaks out after me into the hallway.

This woman is so intent on chasing me, she gets halfway down the hall before realizing she's still naked. She turns and runs back to the room. I push the button to call the elevator. Finally it arrives, and there are lots of people in it. I do my best to compose myself and tuck into the far corner. I have escaped. I take a deep breath. As the doors start to close, her skinny arm pokes in and the doors bounce back open. She slinks on, still dressing herself, and she's staring right at me. Everybody looks at her out the corner of their eyes as she tries to shove in next to me. The instant the doors open, I push my way through the people and take off running like an Olympic sprinter toward the bus, but she's still running after me. The bodyguards finally catch on and intervene so I can get safely onto the bus. I look out the tinted windows at her, glad she can't see me. Security is restraining her as she wrestles with them, trying to get on the bus.

As our fame grows, so does my fear for my safety. It isn't thrilling or exciting to have a woman you don't know and have no interest in behave so aggressively. I feel violated. If a man had behaved the way she did, it would be called sexual assault. Because of this woman's unhinged behavior, and the behavior of other fans over the course of the tour, I opt to carry a personal weapon. Nobody in the band can go anywhere without bodyguards to protect us.

The shows gross more than $100 million, and while the band could keep going and we could surely do an international tour, Prince is ready to move on to the next album. He plans to outdo *Purple Rain,* but I cannot imagine anything bigger than what we've been experiencing; we are at the pinnacle of success, and I am recognized everywhere I go, even after the tour is over.

Back home one night, my brother and I return from a late-night party to my house in Eden Prairie. As we pull into my driveway, I see that the automatic outside lights aren't coming on, and it is dark out here, thirty miles south of Minneapolis and away from the city's glow. My current ride is a silver convertible Corvette, and I keep a pistol-grip, twelve-gauge shotgun behind the seat. We hop out of the car and start our way up to the house. But I stop and freeze. Someone is approaching us—a shadow that is coming closer and closer, moving furtively. My heart is jumping out of my chest because I am unarmed; I've left the shotgun in the car. My brother and I stand stock-still, coiled and ready to fight for our lives. I am certain this intruder is going to kill us. I imagine this is going to be the night we die. Then a voice in the dark addresses us.

"No, no. I'm sorry, I'm so sorry. I didn't mean to frighten you. I'm just a fan, just a fan!"

"YOU STUPID ASSHOLE! YOU CAN'T COME TO A PERSON'S HOME IN THE MIDDLE OF THE NIGHT." I am yelling and angry. "JUST BE-CAUSE YOU'RE A FAN? I USUALLY CARRY A GUN. YOU COULD BE DEAD RIGHT NOW!"

I just let him go. I don't even file a trespassing report. I can see he is genuinely sorry for his actions. It is a wake-up call to me to think about the dangerous combination of my fear and the serious responsibility of owning a gun.

After this incident, I have gates installed.

Another time, I leave First Avenue with Sir Casey Terry from Mazarati, and as we walk to my recently purchased white Ferrari, we see a large Ford F50 with monster tires and two Confederate flags hanging from the back bumper. There are four guys in the bed of the truck. Suddenly, three guys jump out of the cab, wielding crowbars. They are walking toward us.

"Yee-ha!" one of them yells. "We gonna whoop some nigger ass tonight!"

These guys are of the mistaken opinion that they're in Al-abama, or maybe Mississippi, and it's clear they have a prob-lem with two black men getting into a Ferrari. Terry flips out a switchblade. While it is impressive, we are ridiculously out-numbered. This is not going to end well.

"Is there a problem here?" It's Screamer, Mazarati's gui-tar player. He walks up from behind us, hollering at the good ol' boys. As it turns out, he has taken his Magnum 357 from wherever he hides it and is showing it to our would-be attack-ers. There is no mistaking the shiny glare from his heater. He's ready to peel back some lead even at the slightest suggestion that he's bluffing. Now they are outnumbered by six rounds of bullets and the three of us.

"Is there a problem here?" Screamer yells again.

"No, no, we were just looking for chicks to get busy with, and thought these guys would know where we could get some action," one of them replies. They can't be sure of just how crazy Screamer might be. We call him Screamer because of the way he makes the guitar scream. He already looks unpredictable, and with a 357 toaster in his hand, he is even more intimidating. The guys slowly back up, jump into the truck, and take off.

Around this same time, I am producing a girl group called Mercedes, and whenever they're in town, they stay at my house. These young women are beautiful, and they like to sunbathe in the front yard in their bathing suits. I am out of town when I get a call from the guitarist, Nikki.

She is frantic. "A man just tried to break into the house!"

I tell her to hang up and call 911. She tells me that he ran away.

It turns out the guy had knocked on the door, and when Sam (the keyboardist) had opened the door and asked, "How can I help you?" his response was a lewd comment. She went to slam the door closed, but he put his foot in the door and tried to push his way into the house. All five of the ladies had rushed at him and beat on him until he turned and ran. I tell them to call the police and file a report.

They give the officer a description of the guy: chubby, white, five-foot-ten with short blond hair and glasses. The cop tells the girls the same thing I've been telling them: no sunbathing in the front yard where any pervert can see them from the highway. The girls are shaken up enough that they agree to stop.

A year later, I am in my bedroom watching television and

petting my cat Kikki, when she freaks out. The hair on the back of her neck pokes up and she hisses at the window like something out of the movie *Alien*. I turn down the sound and listen. I hear footsteps. Somebody has jumped the fence and is right outside my window. All the lights are out in the house. I turn off the television so the trespasser can't see me. I hit the floor and grab the shotgun I keep under my pillow. I crawl across the floor in the dark to the front door and open it quietly and slowly. In the bright moonlight and with my floodlights behind the bushes, I can see everything, but the intruder can't see me. I creep down the front step of my house. That's when I hear footsteps coming closer. I peep out from behind the dwarf mugo pine bushes and I see a man smoking a cigarette heading straight for my front door. All the fear and paranoia that's been building up over the years fill my belly and I jump up, filled with adrenaline, and yell, "FREEZE, MOTHER F—, OR I'LL BLOW YOUR EFFIN' NUTS OFF!" I charge him and shove the barrel of my gun straight into his family jewels.

He throws his hands up in the air and at the same time pisses his pants. He begs me not to shoot him.

"What are you doing here?"

He has no answer. I am so shaken and angry that without thinking I tell him to run and to not stop running or I will unload the heat from my toaster. He takes off running as fast as he can.

A few days later, I am so mad at myself for not calling the police to get him, lock him up, and charge him, because he fit the description of the guy my young women guests described earlier. I suspect he hoped to catch one of them home alone, thinking I was out. It is terrifying to think what might have happened.

Because of the frequency of this type of brazen behavior from strangers, I have come to rely on guns to feel safe. I am always looking over my shoulder and never sure who is lurking in the dark. Being famous, it turns out, is not for the faint of heart.

THE CARROT AND THE HAT TRICK

WE ARE NEARING THE END of the Purple Rain Tour, and the personal attacks from Prince are becoming more frequent.

People like what I do onstage, and as I get closer with the audience, I sense that Prince doesn't like it. Am I imagining that I'm in the dark onstage, that he is trying to eclipse whatever light I might be shining?

One night I'm watching videos of the shows and I see it, right there on the screen. I have not been imagining it. I see that I am in complete darkness. I point it out to the lighting director.

"Why am I disappearing from the shows?"

He says he'll take care of it.

Over the next few nights, I notice there is no change. I am backlit, but there are no lights on me from the front. One night, while watching the videotapes of the show with Prince, I ask, "How come I'm suddenly in the dark?"

He tells me it's probably an oversight. So I decide to go back to the lighting director and ask him why he still has me in the dark most of the show. His response startles me.

"Mark, I was instructed to pull the lights off you," he responds quietly.

I'm not upset with him. We have the same boss. I know how it goes.

I am angry with Prince, but I justify his behavior. *This is his world, his creation, and I'm just here to help him achieve his dream. I have a choice here: if I don't like it I can always leave.* I focus on the paycheck and the fat bonus he's promised us at the end of the tour. I also concentrate on the personal projects I have in the works. "You'll never have to worry about money again," Prince has always promised. "Stick with me." And I do. I tell myself that I don't care about the money because I love the craft. I love making music, and I reason that in the grand scheme of things, this musical journey with Prince will all be worth it.

I'm not entirely sure I believe the things I'm telling myself.

Our last show of the tour is in Miami at the Orange Bowl. It is an epic way to finish out the tour, and it is a phenomenal show. I think we could play another six months and people wouldn't be tired of it. When I think back on our first Rolling Stones concert, it seems like a lifetime ago, and yet it has all happened so quickly for us.

I am excited to get the tour bonus; 1.7 million tickets were sold over six months. I have heard the shows have grossed more than $100 million, and if our bonus is even just 5 percent of that revenue, it would mean $5 million for the band. I plan to buy my mother a house and look forward to doing things to help out my family. There is love and energy backstage after the show. The Revolution has become a family and our bond is unbreakable. That's my belief.

The accountant enters with envelopes and begins to pass them out, and my heart is hammering so fast I'm not sure I can handle seeing so many zeros. I see the others opening their envelopes. It is overwhelming, and I don't want people to see what I look like when I open mine. I duck into a corner and remember

Momma Vader's words: "Mark, hang in there and remember, this is a chance of a lifetime. It will pay off." I slowly tear open the envelope, keeping my eyes closed tight when I pull out the check. I want to savor this incredible moment. I sneak a quick, tiny peek and see $, then a 1, a 5 . . . my heart is thundering now and everything is blurry as I look up to the heavens.

Is this $1.5 million? Oh my God.

I look back down at the check and drop it on the floor. I am in utter disbelief. Did I really see what I saw? Were there only three zeros? 1-5-0-0-0? I pick it up and look at it again. The check is for $15,000. *Fifteen. Thousand. Dollars.* I have worked a grueling schedule of ninety-eight shows from November to April. I have worked hours upon hours before every show on new material. I have been promised merchandise sales. And this is my bonus. What should be joy turns to disgust. I look around, and everybody has confused looks on their faces. These are our bonus checks, but the room is completely silent. I don't know what is going on, but I'm furious.

I pick up my check from the floor and head off in search of Prince. I need an explanation. I knock on the door. He doesn't answer. I knock again, harder. I know he's there.

"It's Brown, open up." My voice is calm. I breathe deeply, remind myself that he is my brother, and assume this must be some sort of a mistake.

He lets me in.

"What is this, Prince?" I ask, waving my check in his direction. "You told me, you *promised* me I would be taken care of—and you give me a check for $15,000? I heard Michael Jackson gave his band members a million each!"

Prince looks at me and calmly replies, "I don't know anything about it. You need to talk to the accountant about that. I don't handle the money."

I am completely deflated. I feel betrayed, used, stupid. Not only has he not given what he promised for this tour, but I have also helped to create material for the next two albums. Much of the music from *Under the Cherry Moon* is going to be used in another movie he is planning. And I'm already pretty certain he doesn't plan to give me any credit for writing. *We've created a monster.* I've been so gullible. I head over to the door.

"I trusted you," I say to him before walking out.

He doesn't say a word in response.

# # #

Thanks to the Purple Rain Tour, Prince has all the funds he needs to build his dream studio: Paisley Park. The project occupies all his time, which is good, because I am free to do whatever I want at this point. I'm free to put all my focus on my band Mazarati. I don't want to hang on to the anger I have for my mentor. It was a gamble, and looking on the bright side I know I helped create something great. I was part of it, and I am proud of my contributions to something that will be written in history. It's time to just move on. I am young, with much to learn still, and I'm eager to get my own things started. Part of me is also still naively hopeful that he will make good on his word—that he'll do right by me. I have been raised to trust that a person's word is their bond.

I start work on Mazarati's demo, intending to shop it to some record companies. I manage to get some headway going with the local media, and the band is starting to build momentum. People still refer to the person behind Mazarati as The Shadow, which suits me just fine, because I don't want Prince to know about the band. I want some big labels to check them out, so I get them a booking at First Avenue and design and build an elaborate set for them. It is made to look like a back alley, with brick walls, graffiti, garbage cans, street lamps, and newspapers thrown about. (Later, Prince would use my set idea for *Sign O' The Times*.)

The show sells out immediately and is a huge success. This new phase of my life is ready to launch.

A few months later when I'm in Los Angeles on business, Prince calls. I need to make my living as a musician and decided to go to France to work on his next film, *Under the Cherry Moon*. I think he's calling to tell me about when we're leaving and some details about his plans for the project. Instead, he tells me he's picking me up in his limo.

As we drive around the city, he starts out by offering a lame excuse about the bonus debacle, then moves on quickly to dangle a fatter, juicier carrot in front of me—telling me to stick with him because he has huge visions and plans for this next film and album. He's talking to me about life and money, and I'm listening because I know I've got my own thing going now, and I'm fantasizing that *maybe*, if I really want to, I might just tell him, "No." But then he drops a bomb.

"I know you have a band called Mazarati."

I don't say a word. My heart is thumping so loud in my chest he can probably hear it. I'm mad and yet also relieved that it's out and he knows. I've been doing some producing for record labels and even some commercial jingles, but I'm going to need more money, and he's my best source of income.

When he breaks the long silence, I am astonished by what he says.

"Mark, we need to stick together. We're brothers and we need to have each other's backs. I know you're here in LA shopping for a record deal for Mazarati, but you should put them on Paisley Park's label. They would be the first band on the label.

You'll have all the access you need to record your other groups, too, and you and I can produce all sorts of music together. *We* built Paisley Park. It took all of us to accomplish this. Paisley is yours, too."

This carrot is so tantalizing, but I am also skeptical.

"So, I would have full access to Paisley and all the studios?" I want him to confirm that what I've just heard is true.

"It is your home."

I am in shock . . . this is such exciting news. This is the best thing for the band, and with this generous offer he's making up for the bitter disappointment I felt at the end of the Purple Rain tour.

I take the bait.

I sign Mazarati to Paisley Park Records. I have most of their album completed at the time. I am still pretty new at producing. This is going to be a big record for the guys, but it's still missing that signature hit song. Prince puts his genius into action and comes up with "100 MPH." Just the jam we need to launch the album.

When the album is almost complete, Prince gives me a cassette tape to listen to. He wants me to consider it for Mazarati. It is just a vocal with a guitar, and it sounds like something you'd hear being sung around a campfire. A blues-folk vibe. The lyrics are "You don't have to be beautiful, to turn me on." I don't like it at all, and the band hates it. It feels like he's thrown us a left-over scrap that he doesn't want because it's unusable.

"What are we gonna do with this, Prince?" I lament. This sucks. And I have to save face with the band and figure out something to do with this. I determine that if he is hell-bent on us putting this song on our album, then I'm gonna put some Brown stank on it and see if we can make something of it. David Rivkin is the engineer and co-producer with me, and he agrees we need to do something to make the song work. So I rebuild the song from scratch and put a groove behind it. It starts to sound even better when David puts this Keypex trick on it by looping the guitar channel through the gate, triggering it with the hi-hat. And just like that, we have a jam on our hands. "I just want your extra time and your . . . kiss." I *know* we've got a hit song for Mazarati. The guys finish putting vocals on the song, and it is a masterpiece. We're listening to the playback and we're all incredibly amped by how good it sounds. We've turned this song into a bona fide winner.

And then Prince walks in.

He gives his signature little sideways smile-smirk.

"What are you guys up to?" He's been listening to the song, and I can see the wheels are turning in his brain.

I tell him we're going to take a dinner break but will be back in a few hours. He tells us he wants to work on it and takes the two-inch tape the music is on to Studio A. When we get back, I tell the guys I'm going to check in with Prince to see where the tape is and see what he's come up with. The guys are superexcited about "Kiss," and we're sure that whatever Prince does will only make it better. I go into Studio A and I hear the track playing. He starts the song from the top and he's added a guitar riff to start it off. It's not what we had, but I love it. When the vocal comes in, it's Prince's falsetto voice singing, "You don't have to be beautiful . . ." I know this is going to be a major hit song for Mazarati.

But now he wants the song back.

"You need to trust me on this, Mark. 'Kiss' will be a *much* bigger hit with us."

"Us?" I ask.

"Yes, with my name, it will be a bigger hit. You should let me put this on the *Parade* album. Don't worry, I'll take care of you this time. Just think, you'll have a writing and producer credit on a *huge* hit song."

I know in my bones this is gonna be a song that people will love. He offers to manage all the credits and publishing rights, points, intellectual property rights—all of it. I know nothing about any of this, because I'm young and still figuring out how all this works, but he tells me to trust him.

When I return to Studio B to tell Mazarati about this change of events, they are not happy. They are really upset with me because they've all contributed to the song and it's solid.

"We already had a good album." I try to reason with them. "It was just a filler track anyway." I point out that we've finished their first album, and I urge them to look forward to their national tour as the first band signed to Paisley Park's label.

It is an exciting time for me, but things are moving fast. I don't have the time to learn all of the important aspects that I've found myself dead smack in the middle of as related to the music biz. I don't understand the legalities of putting a group out, but I do what I can: I hire a manager, a lawyer, and form a production company. I build a sound company so they are equipped for road life. We have a twenty-six-foot truck with all the equipment the guys need for a dynamic tour. I finance everything on my own. I spend about $500,000, but I'm certain this is a foolproof investment because the guys are in Prince's camp, and all eyes in the industry are on them. Their first song "100 MPH" comes out and it's a hit. Mazarati starts to chart on *Billboard*, and we're off to a good start.

In March, I am in Los Angeles taking some time off from work. I'm watching music videos and relaxing at a friend's house when I discover that Prince has made a video of "Kiss" with Wendy. I am dumbstruck because I have not been told of the song's release, or that a video was being made. I immediately contact Prince, asking why he hadn't told me he was going to shoot a video of our song. He says he didn't need my permission to release this as a single.

When I finally get my hands on the album, my name is nowhere to be found, except for a credit for Hand Claps. I am furious. We had an agreement. In our conversation he told me I was to be given co-writing credit for the song "Kiss."

Prince tells me, "It's a mistake," and he'll look into it.

He assures me I'll be taken care of and sends me off to Nice, France, to work on the *Under the Cherry Moon* movie. I have no idea why I'm going to France for four months. I have one walk-on scene during the song "Girls & Boys" at the end of the movie, and another song I was jamming on at the warehouse that he liked so much he had the band work on it and put it in the movie.

I was never credited for that song either.

Every time I am ready to go home, Prince finds some reason for me to stay. I sit in my hotel room most of the time, bored out of my mind. I make some friends there, and they try to teach me French. I want to get home to work with Mazarati and my girl group Mercedes. I have also discovered a talented black Italian kid named Georgio Allentini, who I'm working with on his solo project. It's not easy communicating across the globe; long-distance calls are expensive and inefficient, and working with different time zones is challenging. I finally break free from France and get back to the States. I have work to do with my bands, Prince has a world tour in the works, and I'm ready to start rehearsing.

Suddenly, everything comes to a screeching halt.

There was a reason Prince kept me in France for so long.

THE BITTER TASTE

WHEN THE PLANE LANDS at the Minneapolis–St. Paul International Airport, I am happy to be home. I am thrilled to be able to sleep in my own bed again. It's not long before the phone starts ringing off the hook. I don't even want to answer it, I am so tired. I am suffering from a bad case of jet lag, but I figure I had better get back to work and start catching up with everything that's been going on since I was gone. I've heard Mazarati was on tour, but missing dates and having serious issues on the road with the members. In speaking with one of the band members, Tony Christian, I learned everything that had been going on since I had been away: they were flown out to LA and put up in hotels; they had been rehearsing for a good month before they were sent out on tour by Paisley Park (or should I cut to the chase and say Prince?); he had changed their show around and tried to get rid of the lead singer; I was also told he wanted Christian to leave the group, bleach his hair blond, and wear a skirt and call himself something else. Prince said he would put together a new group with him and let the band fall apart. I am thinking to myself, *This can't be true.* And who's paying for their hotel stay in LA for a month and the rehearsal studio? This would cost a fortune, and I know they don't have the budget for it, nor did I approve it. I refuse to believe Christian and dismiss what he tells me.

We are getting ready for the release of the new movie *Under the Cherry Moon*. I am told we are going to do a huge premier party in Sheridan, Wyoming, due to an MTV contest, and Mazarati is going to be the opening act, followed by Sheila E, and of course us—Prince and The Revolution. This is going to be a big break for Mazarati, and I will be able to move in a different direction. The problem is that things are getting really weird in the purple camp with me.

I show up to our first day of rehearsals for the upcoming tour, and I notice that my bass rig is in a different place. My microphone stand is set up way in the back next to Bobby Z and in front of me is a large purple piano. I have to literally squeeze between the drum riser and the piano to get to my new home onstage. *Hmmmm,* I am thinking, *what in the devil is going on here?* Directly in front of me and the piano, where I usually stand onstage, are three microphones. Two of the guys who used to be on security detail for Prince are dressed in black and white standing there with Jerome Benton, Morris Day's right-hand man from The Time. All three now take my place at the front of the stage. I am truly bothered at this point, so I walk up to Prince and ask why I am being pushed to the back of the stage with these guys standing in my place.

He looks down and then says, "Whose stage is this, Mark?" As we start our first day of rehearsal, I know what this is about. It's time to show me who's in charge, whose house this is, who signs the checks around here. I've been making moves and now it's time to deflate me.

I have representation now. I call up my newly hired manager, Craig Rice, and tell him I am finished. I am going to quit the band.

The next time I see Prince, I walk up to him and say, "I quit!"

Enough is enough. Prince is right—it is his house, this is his production. I am just the bass player. It is a hard reality check for me, because I feel at the same time that I am something more than just someone he's using up.

I thought we were family. I thought he said we were always going to be boys. Didn't he tell me to stick with him and help him build his empire? Didn't he tell me we'd produce albums together on Paisley? Didn't he say, "I got your back, brother?" And didn't he tell me, "One day *you'll* produce *me*"? I am deflated, sad, emotionally tired, and broken. Am I overreacting? Am I being a baby about this? The one who means the most to me says, "No." Momma Vader, my beautiful loving mother who supported me through this incredible ride—even she knows it is time for me to move on.

A few days later I get a call from Prince asking me to come back. I explain to him how I am feeling. "You promised me you had my back! You talked me into turning down multiple deals with top artists to stick with you! You took my band, my hard work over the years, and put them on your label only to try and dismember them! You lied and insulted me when you gave me that pitiful tour bonus after years of hard work to help you get to where you are! We are your band, your friends, and your family! No, I can't come back this time."

He starts dangling the carrot again, but I say, "No! No! No! You cannot do that to me anymore. I'd rather be poor than suffer defeat like this. Promise after promise you rob me of my self-worth! My self-confidence! No!"

Later, my manager has a long talk with me, explaining what this next phase can do for Mazarati. Everything I have been working so hard for—it all seems within reach. He is helping me to get back on track and see the bigger picture. So I decide to do this last tour, but under a separate contract. I tell Prince I want $X per show and after the tour is over I'm finished. He agrees to my terms and the contract is signed. I am now for the first time just a hired gun to hold down the bottom. I will no longer interact with him on stage. I will be a bass player for hire.

The Parade tour gets on its way with a bang. We sound like a Vegas act on the road. It is big, with at least thirteen band members joining The Revolution onstage: a huge production bringing in millions of dollars. All the promises were—and are—just words to me. I know The Revolution doesn't know I am now under contract. I am forbidden to tell them of this agreement. Mazarati opens the show at Cobo Hall in Detroit. It is a huge show with so many screaming fans. Mazarati is so happy because they feel they hit the big time. This was the biggest crowd they had ever played for. They all hug me and thank me for helping them and being their mentor. I am proud of them.

After that first show, suddenly they are removed from the tour. Prince sends them off on their own to do smaller circuits, and I can't understand why. I am furious. The sad part about it is I'm not notified of this until after they are sent off. They start off on a small U.S. tour to fend for themselves with no support money. I have to put up more than $100,000 of my own money to support them, and by the time their tour is over, it ends in disaster. I am doing a world tour and am completely out of touch with them. I have to entrust them to the record label. It is a long, long tour with so much traveling. In the short spurts of time I have between countries, I try to take care of business and check on the group, but I'm not hearing any good news about them. They aren't doing well at all.

As our tour comes to an end we land in Japan and play the

Yokohama Stadium. It is packed with excited fans. I started out this journey in a stadium for my first big show with the Rolling Stones and now end it in a stadium with Prince and The Revolution. We are a huge success.

It isn't long before Mazarati comes off the road and disbands. My time away from them took its toll. They were put on the road with no money and were literally starving. I hear that the bus driver even used his own pay to bring them home to Minneapolis. Christian's story is starting to become more and more believable. I can't understand what happened to them out there. To top it off, drugs and alcohol have consumed a once battle-hardened band. It's hard to put the pieces of the puzzle together, but it is almost as if they have been set up for failure while their leader, me, was across the sea. They thought that I had abandoned them and left them to fend for themselves. It was all too confusing at the time. I can't put my finger on what the exact cause of their failure was. They even abandoned my truck on the road after it had broken down somewhere out there. I had more than $80,000 worth of equipment on that truck, and I never will discover what happened to the gear. Gone without a trace.

Toward the end of the year, the band is no longer speaking to me. My truck is found abandoned at a parking lot somewhere in Tennessee, I think. It is empty. All my equipment is gone. I can't even file an insurance claim because it was abandoned. It had been missing for months before anyone told me.

I was to collect my final check from my contract with Prince for $50,000, but it never came. I call my manager to please find out why I haven't been paid my last installment for services rendered. He contacts Paisley Park, and they immediately put him in contact with their attorneys, who politely tell us that because of the Artist Contract between Paisley and Mazarati, upon termination of my agreement with Prince, I will have to pay back to Paisley the full amount of what was spent for Mazarati to be flown out to LA to rehearse and for the cost of their rehearsal space. Now, I never sent my group to LA to rehearse, and I never authorized anything, yet I am going to be held responsible for it?

My lawyer says that he had made a mistake. There was a clause in my final contract with Prince that said that if I leave PRN Productions, I will have to pay back this money—get this—to the amount of $50,000. Really? Sounds like this was a setup from the get-go. I am just bamboozled out of $50,000 hard-earned cash. I leave empty-handed. All my years of devoted service and hard work, and to leave with nothing—this is hard to swallow.

I start looking into producing artists, so my manager and I start meeting with record executives and trying to piece together a career where I can survive. I have a very nice studio in my home. I have skills as an engineer, composer, writer, and producer. Things may yet change for me, that's my thinking.

One day I am meeting with the VP of a record label in my dining room when I hear my doorbell ring. I excuse myself and go to answer the door wondering who it could be. I'm not expecting company. To my surprise, it is a sheriff's deputy. Behind him I can see a flatbed truck backing into my driveway. What's going on here?

"What's this all about?" I ask.

"I have here a warrant, and you are hereby served."

I'm thinking, *Served what?*

As I watch him walk away, the flatbed truck is loading up my Ferrari. I have no clue what is going on and my manager grabs the papers from my hands and begins to read. I know I don't owe anything on the car, so why are they taking it?

My manager looks at me and says, "Did you authorize the purchase of equipment at the music store?"

"Never," I reply. I never bought anything there with credit. "Well, it's saying here that you owe the store $15,000, and Karl, the owner, has a judgment against you for the total amount."

What? *That's impossible.* "I've never ever signed or authorized anything from his store."

The really sad thing here is this same guy owns the Ferrari dealership I had bought my Ferrari from, and he somehow convinced a judge to put a judgment against me that I of course was never served. So the time lapsed and I never showed up for court. They had somehow falsified documents, and my signature that proved I was in debt for this gave them an open line of credit and said I was good for it. I had never authorized any of this. I call my attorneys and scream for help on this one.

They say to me, "Mark, our advice to you is to let it go. You can't go up against a judge, especially with these forged documents." They find out the judge is related to Karl and they have put this scheme together.

I go for a second opinion with another attorney and he gives me the same advice. He says, "Listen to me, Mark, you are a young black boy with a lot of money going up against a judge. Even if I take this case, it'll cost you more than what you paid for the car, and I can almost guarantee we'll lose." I get a taste of reality—American justice when your skin is dark in color.

My mother works for the police department now, so she always catches wind of things that are going on in the department downtown. So one day she calls me and she is pretty frantic. She asks me, "Have you sold your car or was it stolen?"

I tell her, "No, why?"

She says, "On the bulletin board in the basement there's a picture of a car that looks just like yours, and it's set for auction tomorrow afternoon!"

I explain to her what has happened and she just cries. She is so angry but knows a typical story is about to unfold for her young black son in a society that condones this kind of injustice. I have been fighting hard in a losing battle and come to grips with the fact that my Ferrari, a dream car, is being taken from me just like that.

What can I do? Nothing but sob at home in disbelief that this could happen to anyone, let alone me.

It's a Friday evening when this so-called auction takes place. My mother says, "There's no address or any kind of information as to where this auction is. I don't know what to tell you, son."

The following Monday she calls me because the bulletin announced the car has been sold at the auction to none other than Karl. The really sad part is it's been sold for five dollars. I still have to pay the judgment of $14,995 for the equipment I never authorized. It is a turning point for me. Something changes in me that year, and I never will look at the world through innocent eyes again. It is a rude awakening for me that I live in a world of filth, greed, and deception.

Broke and down at heart, I decide to run away for a while. I board a plane leaving for Hawaii, where I have a friend, Miguel, who is filming a movie over there. I just want to hang out for a while. Sitting on the airplane, the young lady next to me asks if she can take a picture with me. I'm like, sure. Even though I am a star in the eyes of many fans, I am completely deflated and feel like it was all a ruse. Everything I had invested my life in has turned to fake. Everything I had going for myself has been taken from under my feet, and there is nothing I can do about it.

While in Hawaii, I have much-needed time to do nothing but ponder over all the pathways and winding roads I have traveled to this point in my life. Now at a crossroads, broken down in spirit, and feeling very insecure about my future. I haven't a clue of where I am to go from here. I do feel *free*, however. I am free of all the lies, deceit, backbiting, and underhanded business practices I had to deal with for years. It is like a breath of fresh air.

I decide to take a crack at surfing. I go to the beach, rent a board, and follow all the surfers out. I do exactly what they do. I try. Paddling out, I notice the waves are much bigger than they look from the shoreline. They tower over me at least ten or twenty feet. As a wave approaches, I notice the real surfers shove the noses of their boards under water and swim under the wave so they can get past the swell. I figure, *Hmmmm, it looks easy: let me give it a try.* As the wave approaches me, I try to dip under the wave and swim beneath it, but the power of the wave is so strong it hits the tip of the board with great force— and then the board hits me hard.

Ouch! All I see is blood in the water. The waves are so strong, they just wash me right back up on shore. I lay there looking up at the beautiful blue sky and begin to laugh as my busted lip swells up.

A lifeguard comes over and asks if I am all right. He looks at my lip and says it isn't severe. I tell him I am new at it, but I'm not going to quit. He gives me the green light and I head back into the water. I am determined to get past the break. As a large wave approaches me, I forcefully push the nose of my board downward and swim like a fish. I do it. I pop up on the other side of that huge swell. *This is easy*, I think. I still have to figure out how to stand up on this thing and ride it back in. I find myself at least fifty yards out.

I just sit on my board, letting the swells go right past me. It is an incredible sight from the backside of a large wave. All I see is a mountain of water pushing forward and crashing into the shoreline. This is my moment—I start to paddle forward so I can catch the wave. My surfboard starts to pick up speed, and I figure I had better figure out how to stand up on this thing. It all happens so fast. As I am about to stand, the board jets out at ultra-high speed, and I find myself twenty feet in the air with no board underneath me. I don't even have time to think about what is about to happen. I crash into the side of this massive wave, and it throws me about like a rag doll. As I hit the water below the wave, it body-slams me to the bottom of the ocean and drags me along the rocks and then spits me out on to the shore.

The force is so intense that the board is no longer attached to my leg. I am lying there in a daze. The lifeguard runs over to me to see if I am okay. I clearly am not. I have cuts all over my body from the rocks on the ocean floor, and I am bleeding. I begin to laugh hysterically as I realize I could have lost my life just then. Clearly, surfing is not for me. The lifeguard tells me I should stick to boogie boarding. At this point, however, I am finished. I have been beaten up one too many times. So I just lay in the sun all day until I see evening coming on, then go back to my hotel. It is a peaceful trip. One I truly need. I think I found myself on that beach.

As I head back to the mainland, I have a much different attitude about life and how I am going to approach it.

I call my manager, Craig, and tell him I am on my way home and have a layover in LA for a few hours. He says to me, "I want you to stay in LA for a few days. Don't worry about your flight. You need to meet someone very important."

I don't really know what he is talking about, nor do I care right now, but I will give whoever it is a listening ear.

MOVING ON

IT'S AN ENDLESS FLIGHT from Hawaii to Los Angeles. With every hour that ticks by, I am feeling more anxious about this mysterious meeting Craig has set up. *I don't even have a demo tape,* I think. This is not how I'd thought things would play out. I'd imagined making a name for myself in Los Angeles as a music producer, since that was what I'd been doing all along, in addition to playing with The Revolution. My plan had been to get back into my studio and put together a demo package to professionally present myself so I could be considered by another label. I look out the plane window at the clouds, contemplating my future.

I'm worried.

Without any revenue flow, I'm not sure how I'm going to cover the cost of making a demo. I know I can use my state-of-the-art home studio—it's got all the bells and whistles—but the electric bill to use it is sky-high. It gets so hot in my studio, I nickname it The Skillet. (Later, I will create a production company called Skill-It.) Hiring a top-notch engineer and paying for the multitrack tapes are going to be expensive.

By the time I land at LAX, I'm wide awake and thrilled to be back in Hollywood.

I meet up with Craig, and as we drive to our appointment we catch up on what's been going on in Hollywood. He isn't telling me where we're going or who we're seeing. When we pull up to our destination—a large building on Sunset Boulevard—Craig can't stop smiling. We go inside and step into an elevator. Craig hits a button, and by now he is positively grinning he is so pleased with himself. I understand why when the elevator doors open and we step out into a beautiful lobby. I see where we've landed.

Our appointment is with Motown Records.

Every record company has a gatekeeper, or receptionist, and if you don't have credentials, you ain't gettin' in. But here they are waiting for me with open arms. Turns out, I have more credentials than I realize. The receptionist even greets me by name. A woman named Debbie introduces herself. She's an A&R director for Motown who explains to me that she has been looking for me. She has a catchy smile and dimples. She's friendly and upbeat, and we hit it off right away. She gushes a bit, telling me she's listened to demos I've made for other artists, and they like what they hear. It's a little embarrassing in the moment but such a balm to my wounded ego. This is why they've invited me to meet and talk with them. I'm all ears, and somewhat in disbelief that this is really happening. "Berry Gordy will want to meet with you, of course," Debbie says matter-of-factly. I cannot believe I'm hearing this—Berry Gordy, the founder of Motown Records. Then she gets right to the point and tells me what the label wants for me—and from me. "We want to sign you as a recording artist, writer, and producer."

We walk and talk as she begins the process of wooing me by taking me on a tour. She works hard at convincing me this is the label I should call home. I am overwhelmed. This legendary label wants to work with me. I am introduced to Lee Young, the vice president of Motown. He is so nice—and one very persistent man. I sense he doesn't want to take no for an answer. He tells me that if Debbie wants me signed, then Lee and Berry will make it happen.

It's all so unexpected. I'm a little wary due to my past experiences and not sure I trust this whole thing. I tell them I need to think about it, because I want to be safe and smart and move slowly with this next critical career step. I want to walk, rather than run, into any decision.

Then Warner Brothers invites me to join their label.

I go back to Eden Prairie, and the calls start coming in from other labels. Craig is making appointments for meetings left, right, and center. It seems my hard work has made an impression, and I am so relieved to discover that I have options. I'm not sure what I want to do, but Mr. Lee Young from Motown seems sure: he calls to tell us he's on a plane headed for Minneapolis from Los Angeles for some business and would like to meet up.

What on earth could he be doing in Minneapolis? Craig and I can only wonder. Of course, we plan to welcome him to our city with enthusiasm.

"I'm on my way over," he tells me when he calls. I didn't know he had my home address. I ask Craig if he knows what's up. He gives a sly chuckle.

"Well, he says he's not leaving until he gets you to sign a contract with Motown."

Craig and I have a good laugh over it—this guy sure is bold! I am surprised by his move; it feels good to be in demand, but I am also thinking that maybe they're making a mistake—or something. I mean, all I am is the former bass player with Prince and The Revolution. I have been the quiet one who never spoke, hidden in the shadows.

Why do they want me? I keep asking myself. It's flattering.

It also feels too good to be true.

The doorbell rings, and when I answer Lee Young stands there with a large bottle of Perrier-Jouët champagne in one hand, a briefcase in the other, and a massive smile on his face. I invite him in.

"Lee, why are you here?" I offer him a seat.

His eyes are locked on mine. "BrownMark," he says in a warm and sincere voice, "I have been instructed not to leave until I have a signed deal with you."

I can't believe it. I can't believe it. Motown, *the* Motown, has come to negotiate with me.

I shoot a look at Craig, and we're both trying not to smile too much—this is an aggressive move.

I don't answer right away but instead show Lee my studio and let him hear some of the music I've produced. We all spend some time together talking music, getting to know each other.

Finally, he tells me he has to be back in Los Angeles and he wants to get down to business. We all sit down in my dining room. He pulls a very large envelope out of his briefcase.

"Let me make this very simple. Your attorney has the agreement and has looked it over and will need you to call him right away." I am surprised to hear this, and Lee continues. "We are prepared to give you an artist deal with Motown and would like you to become one of our producers as well."

Craig does his job and asks, "What kind of money are we talking, for an advance?"

Lee smiles. "Name your price and that's our deal."

I look at Craig in absolute disbelief.

"Name our price?" Craig repeats, not sure what he's just heard.

"Yes, I told you I wasn't leaving without a deal. And I was told to give you what you ask for."

Craig tells Lee that he and I need to discuss this for a few minutes downstairs in the studio. As Craig and I go over publishing figures, and marketing, recording, and development figures, we get a strong sense of what amount to present. But Craig has an idea.

"Lee said to name your price, so let's go really high. All he can do is say no."

Craig made all of this happen, so I opt to follow his lead. I figure he must know what's best. We go back upstairs to meet with Lee.

"So what's the damage?"

Oh wow, here we go, I think. I have butterflies. I know this is a day like the day I met Prince—one I will never forget.

Craig makes some clarifications with Lee and then leaves the room to call my attorney to get the go-ahead. He comes back and asks Lee for the world. It is a substantial amount of money and keeps my publishing deal separate. We are shooting for the moon.

And we get it.

After the deal is signed, Lee grins. "Whew, I was scared you were going to ask for more."

Craig and I look at each other with the exact same thought: *We could have gone with a higher figure!* It doesn't matter, though. Honestly, it has never been about the number of zeros on the check: my measure of success has been the ability to put my talent to work and to live a life of passion—dedicated to music.

And to feel appreciated.

Lee reaches over the table and puts out his hand to shake mine, marking the closing of our negotiations, and the beginning of the next chapter of my life.

"Welcome to the Motown family, BrownMark."

EPILOGUE

I HAVE ALWAYS BELIEVED a goal unwritten is a dream. I have created a plan for every goal I have ever wished to achieve, and I made my dreams a reality.

Writing this book was one of them. Looking back, I recognize just how fortunate I am, in spite of so many obstacles. Things might have gone very differently, had I made choices that were not linked to my dedication to having a successful life. But it would not have happened without a lot of hard work and holding tight to a vision of what I wanted for myself.

And good fortune.

And there was some praying in the mix, too.

Prince and I remained friends, and I always regarded him as family. He was my big brother and loved me in a big brother kind of way. He took a young street kid with ambition and taught me how to play the music game. He toughened me up with lessons that were sometimes harsh and hurtful. My perspective has changed on that relationship, since I have a younger brother of my own. As the years passed, I saw that he was just showing me the way, while trying to make his own way—and doing it the only way he knew how. He was growing up, too. And he wasn't perfect. But he gifted me some magnificent tools.

Something he said I have carried with me throughout my career: "Always blaze new trails." I learned that fear kills success and destroys healthy self-esteem. I learned to avoid negative people with a too-small vision of success. I learned that a friend is someone who encourages and supports ambitions and dreams. I learned to be aware of the damage that fear, jealousy, or bad baggage can bring to a relationship . . . and to release those people from my life. They come in many different shapes and sizes and have even come from within my own household and family.

My advice to an aspiring artist, or to anybody fortunate enough to have found their life's purpose: don't wear a white suit among dirty people. They'll just make you dirty, too.

When I was a boy, I made the decision to become a musician. This led to many choices I had to make. I had to learn how to become a successful musician. Working with Prince was like going to the finest music school in all the land.

Rest in peace, my big brother. I will help pass your legacy on, until we play again.

ACKNOWLEDGMENTS

THIS BOOK IS DEDICATED to my mother, Bernice Brown (1933–2020), RIP.

I thank my family for their love and support through my life journey: Yvette, Michael, Jimmy, Neko, and Miguel Brown.

Thank you to my best friends, Harlan Austin and Chris Boon.

I thank my childhood role models: Ron Austin, Walter (Wally) Bell, Michael (Chico) Smith, and Craig Lawrence Rice. I also thank my Central High music teacher, Mr. James Leon Hamilton, RIP.

I acknowledge the help and contributions of Cynthia Uhrich, Amir "Questlove" Thompson, photographer Demetrius Williams, Terry Washington of Zane Ryder Management, Edwin Breed, Susan Thurston-Hamerski, and Craig McBee.

I owe a special thanks to Carmen Hoover. I couldn't have finished this book without her.

And Prince Rogers Nelson: thank you for all the opportunities you gave me as a young adult.

BrownMark (**Mark Brown**) spent most of his life in Minneapolis and grew up with musicians such as Prince, Jimmy Jam and Terry Lewis, Morris Day, and Alexander O'Neal. In 1981, he made his debut with Prince on the *Controversy* tour and became known for his funky bass playing for Prince and The Revolution. He debuted his solo album *Just Like That* on Motown in the late 1980s with the single "Next Time." He received two Grammy Awards and two American Music Awards for his contributions to the *Purple Rain* movie soundtrack. He has performed with Stevie Wonder and Stevie Ray Vaughan and has shared the stage with Sting, Bruce Springsteen, the Rolling Stones, Q-Tip, and Doug E. Fresh.

Author and award-winning filmmaker **Cynthia M. Uhrich** is the founder of In the Moment Films. Her writing has been published by Smith & Krauss and Freshwater Press, and she facilitates a twice-yearly writing retreat for women in her home state of Minnesota.

Ahmir "Questlove" Thompson is an American drummer, DJ, producer, designer, culinary entrepreneur, music educator, and bestselling author. He is cofounder of The Roots and the bandleader for *The Tonight Show Starring Jimmy Fallon*. He lives in New York.